T0328465

Cambridge Elements ≡

Elements in Ethics
edited by
Ben Eggleston
University of Kansas
Dale E. Miller
Old Dominion University, Virginia

NIETZSCHE'S ETHICS

Thomas Stern

University College London

CAMBRIDGE
UNIVERSITY PRESS

CAMBRIDGE
UNIVERSITY PRESS

University Printing House, Cambridge CB2 8BS, United Kingdom

One Liberty Plaza, 20th Floor, New York, NY 10006, USA

477 Williamstown Road, Port Melbourne, VIC 3207, Australia

314–321, 3rd Floor, Plot 3, Splendor Forum, Jasola District Centre,
New Delhi – 110025, India

79 Anson Road, #06–04/06, Singapore 079906

Cambridge University Press is part of the University of Cambridge.

It furthers the University's mission by disseminating knowledge in the pursuit of education, learning, and research at the highest international levels of excellence.

www.cambridge.org
Information on this title: www.cambridge.org/9781108713320
DOI: 10.1017/9781108634113

First published 2020

A catalogue record for this publication is available from the British Library.

ISBN 978-1-108-71332-0 Paperback
ISSN 2516-4031 (online)
ISSN 2516-4023 (print)

Nietzsche's Ethics

Elements in Ethics

DOI: 10.1017/9781108634113
First published online: January 2020

Thomas Stern
University College London
Author for correspondence: Thomas Stern, t.stern@ucl.ac.uk

Abstract: This Element explains Nietzsche's ethics in his late works, from 1886 onwards. The first three sections explain the basics of his ethical theory – its context and presuppositions, its scope and its central tension. The next three sections explore Nietzsche's goals in writing a history of Christian morality (*On the Genealogy of Morality*), the content of that history and whether he achieves his goals. The last two sections take a broader look, respectively, at Nietzsche's wider philosophy in the light of his ethics and at the prospects for a Nietzschean ethics after Nietzsche.

Keywords: Nietzsche, ethics, evolutionary ethics, perspectivism, will to power

ISBN: 9781108713320 (PB), 9781108634113 (OC)
ISSN: 2516-4031 (online), ISSN 2516-4023 (print)

Contents

Introduction

Any author who wants to write about Nietzsche faces a number of challenges. The most striking is surely Nietzsche's style, which makes it difficult to find a firm footing. Amongst other things, his writing is exuberant, distractible, bet hedging, shape-shifting, grandiose, littered with familiar and unfamiliar names, often overtly fictional and, in turns, attractive and repulsive. Then again, at least it is finite. A second challenge comes from the seemingly limitless quantity of secondary literature: commentary, biography, philosophical exploration of his themes, not to mention tertiary literature: writing *about* writing about Nietzsche – all of which, taken as a whole, lends the impression that everything must surely have been said. These two challenges are especially daunting when combined, for the implication is that interpreting Nietzsche's philosophy is an impossible task that, in any case, has already been completed.

To my mind, though, a third challenge takes centre stage. It is the problem of not knowing which prejudices, faint associations, schools of interpretation, hopes and dreams or thorough-going enmities the reader brings with her or him to this man and his ideas. One can note, by all means, that there are many helpful explorations of, for example, Nietzsche and Nazism (Aschheim 1992, 232–71; 315–30; Golomb and Wistrich 2002), the Jews (Holub 2016), post-modernism (Koelb 1990; Gemes 2001), the legacy of his sister (Holub 2002), his illness (Volz 1990; Huenemann 2013), his philosophical and intellectual context (Small 2001; Brobjer 2008; Holub 2018) and his reception and influence (Aschheim 1992; Higgins and Magnus 1996, 281–383; Reckermann 2003; Woodward 2011). These are useful places to start if you think that Nietzsche was a proto-Nazi, or, conversely, that he wrote nothing troubling or offensive and was completely misunderstood and unjustly appropriated by the Nazis with the aid of his evil Nazi sister; likewise, if you think that he certainly died of syphilis, or that he was a visionary whose ideas arose free from any intellectual context or influence, or, indeed, a philosopher working with presuppositions and preoccupations more or less identical to our own. But there is something inhospitable about greeting the reader with a blizzard of references. Rather than attempting the impossible task of clearing away any prejudicial associations, I move to what I take to be the most feasible alternative: to be as clear as possible about the aims, method and scope of this account of Nietzsche's ethics.

This study focuses exclusively on Nietzsche's late works – that is, from 1886 until he ceased writing in 1889. More specifically, that means the following texts: *Beyond Good and Evil* (*BGE*), *On the Genealogy of Morality* (*GM*), *The Case of Wagner* (*CW*), *Twilight of the Idols* (*TI*), *The Antichrist* (*A*), *Ecce Homo* (*EH*), the prefaces he wrote in 1886 for his earlier works and, though to a lesser extent, the unpublished notes of this era. Why focus in this way? First, this period includes *GM*, probably Nietzsche's most influential work in contemporary, Anglophone philosophical circles. We will look at this text in some detail, but it cannot be considered in isolation. Of the texts of this period, for example, Nietzsche seemed to place a greater weight on *A*: he spent many years promising a *magnum opus*, and in the end he claimed that *A* was that *magnum opus* (see Sommer 2013, 6.2:3–8). Second, the late works present, relative to some of his earlier works, a clearer, more unified ethical project. There is a distinct position to be explained and consequently, of course, a target at which to aim. This does not make the period in question better than his earlier writings in every respect: in being less definite, the earlier texts are probably more fertile and suggestive. But it does make the late works more suitable for this concise but comprehensive treatment. Third, in addition to presenting a more coherent position, the ethics of the late period are distinctive. There are traces of his late view in earlier writings, and traces of earlier views in the late writings, so one should not expect a perfectly neat division (for an overview, see Stern 2019b). But treating the late works as a distinct body of writing is a helpful point of entry, whereas, conversely, a detailed discussion of similarities and differences across all texts and periods would be disorientating. The virtues of clarity and focus have also determined the precise choice of texts. The work that falls just outside my chosen period – *Thus Spoke Zarathustra* – was clearly considered, by Nietzsche, to be highly significant. It traditionally marks the transitional phase from the middle to the late works. The contested nature and status of *Zarathustra*'s claims, uttered by fictional characters and situated within a fantastical narrative, render it particularly ill-suited to clear exposition (for discussion, see Pippin 1988; Luchte 2008). However, nothing within that text casts doubt on the picture, drawn here, of the works that followed it. In sum: the late works have been chosen because they are more influential and more distinctive in both coherence and content.

There is also a further reason for focusing in this way – one that pushes us towards questions of method. Nietzsche's late ethical view, as presented here, has not yet been set out with sufficient clarity. Even allowing for Nietzsche's writing style, with all its pitfalls, the late ethical position is relatively clear. The late Nietzsche has not deserved the cacophony of differing interpretations that currently threatens to drown out the thinking, and sap away the confidence, of any student who approaches him. Why so many interpretations, if the underlying position is clear? Likely, there are many reasons. But one methodological feature of my approach may be a contributing factor and, in any case, it is well worth highlighting in its own right. I do not see this study as a *defence* of Nietzsche, as though his interpreter were a lawyer in the final court of philosophical arbitration. Nor do I see it as a project of creative reconstruction in which an imagined figure called 'Nietzsche', or an appealing, Nietzsche-inspired philosophy, emerges from a series of present-day conversations. This may sound unremarkable and uncontroversial, even banal. But, in the context of what is now known as 'the History of Philosophy', and of Anglophone philosophical Nietzsche commentary in particular, it is not. Implicitly or explicitly, a great deal of philosophical writing about Nietzsche, and other historical figures, is creative in method and apologetic in aim. It looks to produce the '*best*' Nietzsche (or equivalent figure) – the one most attractive to present-day Anglophone philosophers – and it is willing to do so at the expense of what its practitioners might see as an inflexible, antiquarian or even 'uncharitable' preoccupation with fidelity to the texts and their historical context (on the questionable ideal of charitable interpretation, see Melamed 2013; Stern 2016; for sceptical remarks on the use of text and history as constraints in contemporary Nietzsche scholarship, see Stern 2018).

My own intention is to stay very close to the texts, to read them in the light of what we know about Nietzsche's intellectual background, and to present the philosophical ideas found in them as clearly, neutrally and thoroughly as possible. While I know better than to predict with any confidence what the reader will make of Nietzsche's views, my guess is that the Nietzsche on display in these pages may seem, in places, dated, wrong-headed and extremely unappealing. So, I do not claim that this will be your favourite Nietzsche, only that it is the real one, or at least a great deal closer to him than much of what is currently available. It seems to me that there is a place – a gap in the market, if you will excuse the expression – for a relatively brief, clear, critical exposition of this real, historical Nietzsche's ethics. Insofar as this methodological stance puts me at odds with readers who want a creative, perhaps more appealing but less textually and historically constrained Nietzschean philosophy, then this will prevent us from talking past each other: such readers can conclude, presumably, that they are not interested in buying what I'm selling. Of course, if some readers imagine that fidelity to the text and context produces a very different result from the one presented here, then I hope to persuade them otherwise. If not, at least we can be assured that our disagreement is genuine.

I have chosen to set out Nietzsche's ideas in a manner that is very different from his own. Despite Nietzsche's explicit reproach, I make an attempt at a systematic presentation (cf. *TI* Maxims 26), along with clearer definition of terms and a great deal less flamboyance. I have not forgotten the student who, after years of studying philosophy at university, could hardly believe that Nietzsche was a philosopher because he was 'so much fun to read'. I suspect she would find it easier to believe that this study of Nietzsche was written by a philosopher. It might be suggested that, by presenting his ideas in this way, they are altered in some sense. This, in itself, does not concern me: presumably, readers have chosen to read this analysis because they think a clearer and more focused presentation of Nietzsche's ideas will be useful. Whatever distortion may have arisen, it is a necessary outcome of such a presentation and nothing prevents anyone from going back to Nietzsche's own words.

A more specific charge might be that my presentation of Nietzsche clashes either with some of his alleged doctrines and stances (such as perspectivism or truth-scepticism), or with some of his specific claims about his own philosophical writing. As for the former, we look at perspective and truth-scepticism in more detail, once his ethics have been sufficiently explored (see Sections 7.1, 7.2). As for the latter, we can mention two examples here. First, he is the supposed advocate of a 'masked' philosophy. Perhaps his philosophical ideas are not put forward sincerely, whereas I present his claims as deeply held convictions? Nietzsche does indeed advocate philosophising with a 'mask' and, although that means a number of different things, one of them seems to entail a cautionary note about direct, open communication and defence of philosophical ideas, albeit for very particular reasons (e.g., BGE 25; for discussion, see Stern 2017). In the case of his later ethics, though, his principal experiment – or 'mask', if that is what it is – is thorough and sustained. It is also unique: there is no other 'mask', no rival view in these texts. If you permanently wear the same mask, then, in a sense, that mask just is your face. *Within* the broad framework of his ethical outlook, Nietzsche certainly tries different things out, some of which contradict others. But he does not step outside the framework. Indeed, as we shall see, matters are the other way around: the difficulties inherent in Nietzsche's framework compel him to experiment within it. A second variant of this objection might be, not that the views I present are a 'mask', but that they are exaggerations, which are not intended to be taken seriously or literally. After all, he subtitled one of our main texts, *GM*, a '*Streitschrift*' – a term that, loosely translated, means a 'polemic'. But we should avoid jumping to conclusions. If I write a polemical pamphlet as part of a dispute with a rival, it does not follow that I don't mean what I say, nor that one would be missing the point by taking my claims and arguments seriously. As it happens, in my view, Nietzsche's claims are indeed supposed to be taken seriously, but I do not attempt to persuade the reader on that score. All I mean to demonstrate is that, *if* you take him at face value, then this is what you get. Put another way: *even if* Nietzsche is making exaggerated claims, which are not intended to be taken seriously for some reason or other, then *these* are the exaggerated claims he is in fact making. Of course, it would be up to my opponent to provide an account of what the exaggerations are, and why they are made. I have not yet come across such an account.

Perhaps the best summary of these remarks would be the following: once we have taken the decision to set out Nietzsche's ethics from 1886 onwards as faithfully as possible, only more clearly and systematically than he does, and once we assume that he means what he says, then what follows is the ethical position we end up with.

The study begins by defining and setting out the key features of Nietzsche's ethics (Section 1) and his critique of Christian morality (Section 2). A central tension in Nietzsche's ethics is presented (Section 3) – one that helps us to understand the aims (Section 4) and content (Section 5) of his best-known work, *GM*, and of other, related histories. We can then assess how successful Nietzsche is in achieving these aims (Section 6). We examine some related and apparently conflicting strands of Nietzsche's philosophy (Section 7), ending with some remarks on how to categorise Nietzsche's ethics and, therefore, on what the future of Nietzschean ethics might hold.

1 Nietzsche's Ethics in Outline

1.1 Terminology

To begin with, it will be helpful to distinguish three things: (i) *a morality*; (ii) a particular instance of a morality, which I call *Christian morality*; and (iii) Nietzsche's own *ethics*.

(i) A morality is a particular value system, belonging to a historical group or groups of people, arising among them for contingent reasons that can be the object of sociological study. Nietzsche has various different examples in mind, including Ancient Greek morality, Ancient Israelite morality and Christian morality.

(ii) Christian morality is a particularly important *instance* of a morality, which can provisionally be thought of as Nietzsche's target, as the villain of Nietzsche's story – even if, as we shall see, the situation is more complicated than this provisional characterisation suggests. Christian morality is dominant and highly significant in modern Europe. Christian morality's adherents are not necessarily faithful Christians, nor are all faithful Christians adherents of Christian morality. It is best understood as a technical term in Nietzsche, not as a description of all-and-only Christian believers, but we will shortly explore its link to Christianity (Section 2.1).

(iii) I will refer to Nietzsche's own moral outlook as his 'ethics'. Although 'ethics' and 'morality' are often synonymous in philosophical writing, I give them distinct definitions here because it would be confusing to speak of 'Nietzsche's morality', given (i) and (ii). That is, it would suggest, wrongly, that Nietzschean ethics, like Christian morality, is just another instance of a morality. Once we understand his ethics, we quickly grasp that he does not see things this way (Section 2.5).

Though he clearly distinguished between these three things, this terminology is not Nietzsche's. He can use 'morality' to denote (i), (ii) or (iii). He does speak of 'Christian morality', but in fact he usually refers to Christian morality simply as 'morality' because it is the dominant form: for example, *On the Genealogy of Morality* is really a genealogy of *Christian* morality. He does not use the term 'ethics' at all, in my sense. However, my terminology enables us to set out the situation with greater clarity. For example, Nietzsche often argues that Christian morality is unethical, but he does not think that every morality is unethical. He also holds that ethical activity is Christian-immoral, that is, immoral by Christian standards, though not immoral by the standards of every morality.

Nietzsche's ethics, as presented here, combine a descriptive thesis and a normative command. We begin with the former.

1.2 The Descriptive Thesis: The Life Theory

When Nietzsche looks out at the realm of living things, what he sees is a domain necessarily characterised by power seeking. Organisms and, as we shall see, even *parts* of organisms, seek dominance and control; they look to increase whatever they have and to subordinate or exploit whatever they encounter. It is a shifting, unstable domain: one entity overwhelms, consumes, destroys or annexes another; or it is, in turn, overwhelmed, consumed and so on. Nietzsche does not deny the existence of cooperative behaviour, but he sees it as instrumental – a variety of power seeking, not a counterexample to it.

Power seeking is not merely Nietzsche's characterisation of how living things usually or often happen to behave: it is biologically essential. As Nietzsche puts it, life, when correctly understood, 'cannot be thought without' such a characterisation (*GM* II 11). *Living* and *power seeking* cannot be pulled apart, from the simplest to the most complex life forms.

In expressing this view, Nietzsche often appeals to something like a power-seeking force, which he variously calls 'Life', 'nature', 'will', 'will to life' or 'will to power'. This force accounts for the power-seeking behaviour inherent in the organic realm. I will refer to this force as 'Life', using the proper noun (including in some translated passages) in part to remind the reader that something unusual is being picked out here. I will still speak of 'life' in other contexts, to indicate, amongst other things, the organic realm as a whole, rather than the force that operates through it: thus, for example, one might say that, for

Nietzsche, Life governs all life. But readers should note that the Life/life distinction is not explicit in the texts, not least because all nouns are capitalised in German.

Life is often presented as an independent agent, a person-like entity with intentions (*Absichten*) (*TI* Morality 6; also, *GM* III 16) and interests (*GM* III 11; *TI* Untimely 36) set apart from our own. Life issues 'commandments', for example (*TI* Morality 4), it 'aims at' various outcomes (*GS* 344), plays tricks on us (*GM* II 7) and 'forces us' to do things (*TI* Morality 5, my translation). Life can 'gain advantage' from certain actions or types of people (*TI* Untimely 36). As might be expected, what Life aims at, what it gains advantage from, has something to do with power. So, we can sketch Nietzsche's view as follows: living things are necessarily governed by Life, a force that operates through them to achieve power-increasing ends. In this study, 'the Life Theory' is my name for this view.

In a number of respects, the Life Theory may appear peculiar to the present-day reader. What is the evidence for the theory? What kind of force are we talking about and by which mechanism does it operate? How could this force, 'Life', have its own goals and intentions? We can make the theory less alien by saying something about Nietzsche's sources and motivations; in any case, we need not pretend that the theory is free from ambiguity, nor that it is given adequate philosophical or empirical support in his texts. Ultimately, though, we should not lose the wood for the trees: the Life Theory is *presupposed* by Nietzsche's ethics, and questions about the theory's finer details, and about how he supports the theory, are less pressing than the question of what he needs it for and what he does with it.

We can therefore leave open the question of whether, for Nietzsche, the *inorganic* realm is also characterised by the same force that governs living things. Nietzsche at least entertains this more ambitious thesis (*BGE* 36; *KSA* 13: 14[121]), which had precedent in Schopenhauer, Mainländer and others. But his ethics do not depend on it. Similarly, we need not closely examine the troubling question of how Life has 'aims' and 'intentions'. While Nietzsche speaks of Life as an intentional agent, Life is not a transcendent deity that directs living things from without. For Nietzsche also insists that Life does not, strictly speaking, have conscious and causally efficacious intentions in the way that these formulations suggest (see *BGE* 9 on 'nature'). 'Of course', Nietzsche might say, 'Life does not want things in the way that we typically think of humans as wanting things. Speaking of Life's "intentions" is just a useful shorthand.' What, though, would talk of Life's 'intentions' be short-hand *for*? The answer would be complex: as we shall see, Life is portrayed as a dynamic force, which can be highly creative and tenacious in seeking out quite specific ends. Reducing or naturalising Nietzsche's language of goals and commandments would not be easy. But, simply put, we don't need to worry about this. A study of Nietzschean metaphysics, teleology or biology might work with the texts, thin though they are in this regard, to speculate about his account of the underlying reality. But those interested in Nietzsche's ethics do not have to draw any firm conclusions about the metaphysical status of Life's goals. What matters for us is why he *speaks* this way. He asks us to think in terms of Life's intentions and interests because he is going to categorise human beings, their actions and their values, in terms of whether they work for or against what Life 'wants' (whatever that turns out to mean on a metaphysical level). He will therefore speak of those on Life's team, the 'party of Life' (*EH* BT 4), and those who at least seem to be on the opposing side (*EH* Destiny 8). Whatever the underlying metaphysical or biological commitments of the Life Theory, this is the division it needs to support: for Life or against Life.

To understand how Nietzsche's ethics puts the Life Theory to work, it will be helpful to say something more about Nietzsche's influences. One clue lies in Nietzsche's occasional adoption of the term 'will to life' (*Wille zum Leben*) to speak of Life, a term that clearly points back to Schopenhauer (*A* 18, 50; *TI* Ancients 4–5; *KSA* 13: 16[86], p. 516; 25[1], p. 637; Nietzsche also speaks of '*Lebenswille*', another Schopenhauerian term usually translated either 'will to life' or 'life-will', see *GM* II 11–12; cf. Schopenhauer 2014. Sections 54, 70, 2018, ch. 44). Schopenhauer had argued that something appropriately called 'the Will' was the thing-in-itself, the real, metaphysical basis of the everyday world as we know it. On Schopenhauer's account, this metaphysical entity operates through all living things, ensuring that biological life continues as it is. Schopenhauer often referred to the Will, when at work in the organic realm, as the 'will to life' (Schopenhauer 2014, sec. 54), primarily because it makes organisms pursue survival and reproduction. Our individual, human wills – our individual faculties of wanting or desiring – are the clear manifestation of what this will to life is aiming at on our behalf: hence, a human individual's will is at its strongest, and hardest to resist, in relation to matters of survival and especially the reproduction of the species. (The Will makes parents prioritise their offspring's survival at their own expense, so *individual* survival is not the ultimate goal, even in Schopenhauer, let alone in Nietzsche's development of Schopenhauer.) To speak anachronistically, the will to life programmes our individual wills for its own advantage. The idea of such a will underlying and controlling biological behaviour was, in the wake of Schopenhauer, extremely influential. Nietzsche was not just reading Schopenhauer, but also others who, following Schopenhauer, produced related but alternative versions, wills that had slightly different programming (e.g. Hartmann 1869; Mainländer 1879; for discussion, see Beiser 2016; Stern 2019b).

Note that one can disconnect Schopenhauer's claim about the metaphysical Will – that there is a single thing-in-itself and it is best called 'Will' – from the biological model of a force (called 'will to life') that operates through all living things. This, in essence, is Nietzsche's move: he need not endorse the story about will as metaphysical thing-in-itself, but he maintains that something like the will to life, albeit with different programming, explains the organic realm.

In addition to Schopenhauer and Schopenhauerians, Nietzsche was also drawing, selectively and inventively, on contemporary scientific or at least quasi-scientific literature. His reading and use of evolutionary theory is particularly relevant (see Moore 2002; Sommer 2010; Emden 2014; Brobjer 2016; Holub 2018, 313–59). Nietzsche certainly knew about Darwin, albeit mediated through other commentators. But Darwin's ideas, though influential, were not universally accepted or understood at this time, even within the scientific community (on German reception of Darwin, see Richards 2013; Holub 2018, 322–9). There were other, non-Darwinian evolutionary theories, which did not seem as implausible as perhaps they would now. For example, one contemporary, Wilhelm Roux, argued that a sort of Darwinian struggle for survival is taking place not merely between animals but *within* them, within their organs and their cells, and that life would be impossible without this permanent struggle (Roux 1881; on Nietzsche's reading of Roux, see Holub 2018, 340–3). Another, William Henry Rolph, argued that life is characterised by permanent 'insatiability', even at the cellular level, and therefore by an ongoing, internecine 'war of aggression', in which each element, by nature never satisfied, sought to accumulate as much of the available resources as possible (Rolph 1884, 97; on Nietzsche and Rolph, see Moore 2002; Brobjer 2008, 170–3; Sommer 2010; Emden 2014, 176–83; Holub 2018, 343–51). Generally, Nietzsche brings together ideas of this kind: Life by necessity seeks increase and accumulation; it operates not just between living beings, but within them.

The combination of the Schopenhauerian and natural-scientific contexts led, in Nietzsche, to a 'will', Life, characterised more in terms of power, conflict, insatiability and exploitation than its Schopenhauerian counterpart. Nietzsche is attempting to correct Schopenhauer, for example, when he speaks of 'the true life-will, which seeks power' (*GM* II 11). What he means is: the correct version of the will that Schopenhauer was talking about, namely the one that seeks *power*, not mere survival and stable reproduction of the species. Nietzsche often emphasises that the 'true life-will, which seeks power', can or ought to ensure that certain individuals do *not* survive or reproduce (see Sections 6.2, 6.3).

Context can also help explain some of Nietzsche's vagueness, which he inherits from his interlocutors. Earlier, we noted Nietzsche's references to Life's aims and intentions, together with his official insistence that Life is blind. The same tension is found in Schopenhauer and even in Darwin, who often presents natural selection as an intelligent agent with specific aims. We might now naturally think of (Darwinian) evolution as goalless. In Nietzsche's time, though, there was considerable debate about the extent to which Darwinian theory implied that nature was goal-directed in a more substantial way (Richards 2009; Holub 2018, 328–9).

We are now able to understand why Nietzsche claims, for example, that 'life itself seems to me to be instinct for growth, for continuation, for accumulation of forces, for *power*' (*A* 6, translation altered), that 'the truly basic life-instinct [. . .] aims at *the expansion of power*', that the 'great and small struggle revolves everywhere around preponderance, around growth and expansion, around power and in accordance with the will to power, which is simply the will to life' (*GS* 349). Or, again: 'what man wants, what the smallest part of every living organism wants, is an increase of power' (*KSA* 13: 14[174], my translation; in this study, '[. . .]' indicates that I have omitted some of Nietzsche's text, whereas ' . . . ', without the square brackets, is Nietzsche's own punctuation). In such cases, his ideas, in context, would certainly have sounded less unfamiliar: they are developments and, he thinks, correctives of their contemporary counterparts.

The Life Theory draws, however idiosyncratically, on contemporary philosophy and natural science to posit Life, a Schopenhauerian 'will' of sorts, directing the organic realm – organisms and parts of organisms – towards the pursuit of power, without which they could not live. As an interpretation of Nietzsche's remarks on will to power, the Life Theory has plenty of competitors in the secondary literature. Some of these resemble it to an extent (for readings that agree closely with mine, see Hussain 2011; Holub 2018, 353; Porter 2013 treats some of the same material from a different angle; the account of Nietzsche's ethics given in Katsafanas 2018 bears a more superficial resemblance to the Life Theory, in part due to the emphasis he places on action and drives). To give some flavour of the available materials, one recent analysis lists eleven *categories* of will to power interpretation (Hatab 2019). But in the quotations just given, and in more to come, taking Nietzsche both in context and at his word yields this reading above all others. It also guides us through the aim and execution of his late writings. This does not mean that the Life Theory grounds Nietzsche's ethics *unproblematically*: indeed, my analysis will suggest the opposite (see Section 3.). Moreover, as made plain at the start, the Life Theory need not amount to the interpretation that is philosophically most complex or satisfying to the modern reader. Consider this remark: 'the attribution of what seems to be some kind of metaphysical agency to 'life' [...] seems to me one of Nietzsche's least inspired and most unfortunate ideas' (Geuss 1999, 28). Nothing I say contradicts this statement, but my aim is to show that this attribution runs much deeper than is often supposed – so deep, in fact, that the nature and distinctiveness of Nietzsche's ethics during the period in question is impossible to understand without it.

1.3 The Normative Command: Further Life's Goals!

The most important point to take from the previous subsection was that, for Nietzsche, to be alive is to be a power seeker: it is to be governed by Life, a power-seeking force that can helpfully be described as having goals and issuing commandments. Now, to put it simply, Nietzsche's basic ethical position is as follows: *it is ethical to further the goals of Life and it is unethical to impede them.*

The Life Theory, sketched in Section 1.2, has little inherent connection with an ethics of any kind because it is merely a description of how living things function, a description which is not obviously connected to an 'ought' of an ethical kind. To a contemporary eye, though, a connection would have been obvious. Again, Schopenhauer is key. We saw that, for him, our individual wills are implanted in us by the will to life, such that we further its interests. However – and this is the crucial point for Schopenhauer – *its* interests and *our* individual interests do not align: the will to life is hostile to our interests. For example, the will to life wants human life to continue, so it implants in us sexual desires and the desire to have children (Schopenhauer 2018, ch. 44). These are perfectly natural because the will to life governs nature. But, Schopenhauer argues at length, we would in fact be better off not being natural, that is, not seeking sexual satisfaction and not having children. Most people simply go along with what the will to life wants from them, following their individual desires (which are implanted by the will to life). But the best kind of human life, Schopenhauer claims, is to deny, oppose or frustrate the goals of the will to life, for example by refusing to have sex or reproduce.

Schopenhauer introduced the terms 'affirmation' and 'denial' to describe these different ways of behaving in relation to the Will's goals (Schopenhauer 2014, sec. 60). To 'affirm' the will (to life) is to go along with what it implants in us as values and desires, which make the continuation of life possible. To 'deny' the Will is to struggle against such values and desires. For Schopenhauer, then, we ought to deny the will to life. Simply put, Nietzsche is arguing, contra Schopenhauer, that affirmation, rather than denial, is best. (For an overview of affirmation in the different phases of Nietzsche's writing, and in its Schopenhauerian context, see

Stern 2019b.) As we can see, Life-affirmation, in this context, is not (primarily or typically) a matter of thinking that it's great to be alive. It means acting on Life's orders or furthering Life's goals. On Nietzsche's understanding, affirmation means to increase, seek power, expand, exploit, while Life-denial means the opposite. Nietzsche also refers to Life-denial as nihilism, because the Life-denier, in effect, acts in a way that would bring about the destruction of living things (on nihilism and Life-denial, see *A* 6–7, 11, 58). Life-affirmation also connects with Nietzsche's idea of eternal recurrence, the repetition of all things over and over again – a notion that first appeared earlier in his writing (on the connection, see in particular Stern 2019b, see also Stern forthcoming). Notice that one can hold that being alive is good, independently of whether one acts on Life's orders. A Life-denier might say 'It's great to be alive!' while opposing power seeking and impeding Life. Similarly, some *apparent* Life-deniers might *say* 'being alive is horrible!' as part of a strategy for pursuing power and hence for affirming Life.

We already noted the natural-scientific context of Nietzsche's Life Theory. But Darwinian and other evolutionary ideas were not restricted to descriptive accounts of species development. They were quickly applied to the practical domain in particular ways that Nietzsche sought to reject (O'Connell 2017). Morality, some Darwinians argued, and altruistic morality, in particular, could be explained and justified on evolutionary principles. Darwin had argued along these lines (Darwin 1871, 1:152–77), as Darwinians continue to do (for twenty-first-century variations, see Richards 2017; Ruse 2017). Nietzsche, however, focused more on the influential Darwinian philosopher Herbert Spencer, who argued that (what Spencer called) a 'higher phase of evolution' occurs when 'members of a society [...] give mutual help in the achievement of ends' (Spencer 1879, 19; for Nietzsche's hostility, see e.g. GM I 3; EH Destiny 4; GS 373). On Spencer's account, in other words, more evolved behaviours are more altruistic. Closer to home, Nietzsche's erstwhile friend, Paul Rée, had also claimed, in his *The Origin of the Moral Sensations* (1877), that morality, again conceived as a form of altruism, was an evolutionary advantage (Rée 2003; *GM* P; on Nietzsche and Rée, see Small 2005, 74–91; Janaway 2007, 74–90). Another contemporary ethicist, J.-M. Guyau, was criticised by Nietzsche for his attempt 'to prove that the [Life-denying] moral instincts have their seat in Life itself' (marginal comments, quoted in Brobjer 2008, 91).

Keeping Schopenhauerian denial and evolutionary altruism in mind allows us to see what Nietzsche is doing with both. Although he is not consistent on this point, Schopenhauer (writing, of course, prior to Darwin) generally presents altruism as *contravening* the natural order: the Will encourages us to be selfish at the expense of others, and altruistic activity is therefore a step in the direction of *denying* the Will's goals. One could therefore imagine a philosopher somewhat like Nietzsche, critical of Schopenhauerian denial, who welcomed the new (purported) evolutionary basis of altruism because it drives a wedge between being moral and denying Life: 'altruistic morality turns out to be just what Life wants!', this philosopher could say, 'so altruism is Life-affirming and, contra Schopenhauer, not a step towards Life-denial!' This is the opposite of the route that Nietzsche takes. Instead of accepting that altruism is grounded in biological life, his Life Theory agrees with Schopenhauer's analysis on the point that altruism is anti-Life. So, what to make of those, like Spencer, who attempt to ground altruism biologically? Not only are they wrong about Life, *they look anti-Life, too, just like Schopenhauer* (*GM* II 12). Rolph appealed to Nietzsche precisely because he argued against Spencer in a similar way: on Rolph's account of life as expansion and insatiability, the idea that one ought to limit what one has, or that, in an ethical context, one could respect the equal rights of others by not taking as much as one could, goes against the fundamental conditions of life (Rolph 1884, 61, 120–1, 222–3).

Nietzsche's normative command is: Affirm Life! The 'affirm' part goes against Schopenhauer, who advocated denial. But the *kind* of 'Life' Nietzsche posits is more Schopenhauerian than that of the evolutionary altruists: Nietzschean Life, like Schopenhauerian will to life, encourages egoism and self-expansion, where Spencer had argued that it favours altruism. All in all, both the descriptive and the normative components become more understandable once we see that his contemporaries were trying to show that altruism – a form of Life-*denial*, Nietzsche thought – was biologically embedded: 'even the basic conditions of life are falsely interpreted for the benefit of [Christian] morality' (*KSA* 12: 2[165]).

This analysis enables us to see how Nietzsche builds his ethical arguments. Of course, there is his famous remark: 'What is good? – All that heightens the feeling of power, the will to power, power itself in man. What is bad? – All that proceeds from weakness' (*A* 2). In the same aphorism, he writes: 'The weak and ill-constituted ought to perish: first principle of *our* philanthropy. And one ought to help them to do so. What is more harmful than any vice? – Active sympathy for the ill-constituted and weak – Christianity' (translation altered). This passage gives the general sense that power should be promoted and the weak should perish or be helped to perish. But we get a better sense of his mode of argument from what he calls a 'primordial fact of all history' (*BGE* 259):

[L]ife itself is *essentially* appropriation, injury, overpowering of what is alien and weaker; suppression, hardness, imposition of one's own forms, incorporation and at least, at its mildest, exploitation.

He continues:

> 'Exploitation' does not belong to a corrupt or imperfect and primitive society:
> it belongs to the *essence* of what lives, as a basic organic function; it is the
> consequence of the will to power, which is after all the will of life.

Here, we see Nietzsche setting out part of the Life Theory, describing how Life,
and therefore the organic realm, works. This accounts for his claim, at the start
of the same aphorism, that 'refraining mutually from injury, violence, and
exploitation and placing one's will on a par with that of someone else', when
these are made into general rules for society, reveal 'a will to the *denial* of Life'
(*BGE* 259). In other words, as we can see, power seeking, exploitation, appropriation and injury are so fundamental to being alive – 'the essence of what
lives', 'a basic organic function' – that opposition to them equates to an
opposition to Life. If 'a living thing seeks above all to discharge its strength',
if 'life itself is *will to power*', then opposing such things equates to Life-denial.

Such Life-denying activities may be contrasted with Nietzsche's own, Life-
promoting ethical vision:

> I formulate a principle. All naturalism in morality, that is all *healthy* morality,
> is dominated by an instinct of Life – some commandment of Life is fulfilled
> through a certain canon of 'shall' and 'shall not', some hindrance and hostile
> element on Life's road is thereby removed. *Anti-natural* morality [. . .] turns
> on the contrary precisely *against* the instincts of Life – it is a now secret, now
> loud and impudent *condemnation* of these instincts. (*TI* Morality 4, transla-
> tion altered)

As we can see from this quotation, Nietzsche often equates Life with nature, as
Schopenhauer had done. By 'naturalism in morality', he means a 'healthy'
morality that is on the side of nature, that is, Life. This is what he claims to
find, for example, in Goethe, who 'did not sever himself from life, he placed
himself within it' and in Goethe's conception of Napoleon, who 'dare[d] to
allow himself the whole compass and wealth of naturalness' (*TI* Untimely
48–9). In the late works, Nietzsche speaks with marked frequency of anti-Life
morality as being 'anti-natural'. He complains of 'the utterly gruesome fact that
antinature itself received the highest honours as morality' (*EH* Destiny 7). This
idea occurs again in *A* 24–7, when he praises the 'natural values' promoted by
ancient Israelites, prior to the developments that led to Judaism and Christianity.
The natural, Life-promoting Israelite value system includes a god who supports
their agricultural and military efforts – both being natural or Life-affirming, in
Nietzsche's terms. Nietzsche also praises the Dionysian Greek mysteries, which
affirm sex, birth and hence Life (*TI* Ancients 4–5). We will shortly be looking at
Christianity in more detail, but Nietzsche makes no secret of claiming that it, or

the morality that it inspires, is hostile to sex (*TI* Ancients 4–5) and generally, to nature: '*all* the concepts of the church are recognised for what they are: the most malicious false-coinage there is for the purpose of *disvaluing* nature and natural values' (*A* 38). Indeed, it would be hard to overemphasise the frequency with which Nietzsche, in this period, associates or identifies Christianity or Christian morality with what is anti-natural (e.g., *A* 15, 16, 18, 24–6, 39; *A*'s 'Law' [*KSA* 6, p. 254]; *TI* 'Morality'; *GM* I 16, II 22–4, III 3, 12; *GS* 344; *BGE* 51, 55; *KSA* 6, p. 431; *KSA* 12: 8[3]; 10[45]; 10[152]; 10[157]; 10[193]; *KSA* 13: 14[138]; 15[4]; 15[110]; 17[4]; 23[1]; 23[10]).

We now have a clear sense of what counts as ethical (Life-promoting) and unethical (Life-denying) for Nietzsche, so we can build on the tripartite distinction between (i) *a morality*, (ii) *Christian morality* and (iii) Nietzsche's *ethics*. Nietzsche's ethics combine a biological claim – the Life Theory – with the normative command to affirm Life. When Nietzsche analyses *a morality*, he is ultimately asking how *ethical* it is, whether or not it is Life-affirming or Life-denying, whether or not it furthers or obstructs Life's goals. Some moralities appear Life-affirming, others do not. In the next section, we follow Nietzsche's analysis of Christian morality in these terms.

2 Christian Morality

From what we have said so far, the reader might expect to be told that Christian morality counts as unethical, that it is anti-Life. Indeed, Nietzsche usually argues that way. However, in spite of its clumsiness, we should provisionally adopt a more cautious formula: Christian morality is, according to Nietzsche, *at least apparently* anti-Life. The qualification is required because it will turn out to be important which of two very different things Nietzsche takes Christian morality to be: first, a genuine and effective impediment to Life; second, merely *apparently* anti-Life (e.g., by making anti-Life claims), but *not*, in fact, a genuine and effective impediment to Life. The phrase '*at least apparently* anti-Life' is simply intended to keep both options open until Section 3, where this difference is discussed in detail. First, we examine different forms of Christian morality, beginning with Christianity.

2.1 Christianity as Christian-Moral

'Christian morality' is a label for a particular set of values, which can be held by some non-Christians and rejected by some of Christian faith. But it is not called 'Christian' *arbitrarily*. Following Schopenhauer, Nietzsche generally treats Christianity as encouraging or promoting asceticism. On Schopenhauer's account, asceticism is the '*deliberate* breaking of the will by forgoing what is pleasant and seeking out what is unpleasant' (Schopenhauer 2014, sec. 68, p. 419) and it is the subject of his high praise: the breaking of the individual will entails an attack on the will to life.

Schopenhauer was not inventing the connection between Christianity and ascetic denial. Early, influential ascetics include St Anthony, who retreated into the desert, and St Simeon, who gained notoriety for living on a pillar. On Schopenhauer's view, though, the roots of Christian asceticism are present in the gospels: 'if anyone wishes to come after me', says Jesus, 'let him deny himself [. . .]' (Luke 9: 23; see also Matt. 16: 24). These roots come to fruition through the subsequent actions of the Christian ascetics, saints and mystics. Inspired by St Anthony, monastic communities formed in the desert; 'Rules', codes of conduct, were written to govern their life. In St Benedict's early and influential *Rule*, newcomers would promise, amongst other things, obedience, poverty and chastity (later known as the 'counsels of perfection' in the Catholic Church). Each may, in a general sense, be linked with the deliberate attempt to eradicate one's will. Chastity operates against sexual desire; poverty deprives one of means for desire-satisfaction; obedience or humility ensures rule by the will of another, not one's own. In each case, there is a fairly intuitive link to the frustration of Life's goals, as sketched in Section 1. Of course, even among faithful Christians, a monastic existence is rare. On Schopenhauer's view, and on Nietzsche's, though, it is the central Christian ideal, Christianity's model of the highest and best way of living.

One tool that Christianity uses in its hostility to Life is of particular interest to Nietzsche (again, following Schopenhauer). It presents this world, our world – the only world there is, according to Nietzsche – as both less than real and morally suspect (*EH* Destiny 8). Consider the contrast between life on Earth and life in heaven, that is, between every day, regular, ordinary existence, over which Satan is said to be Lord, versus a better world beyond. In a passage known to Nietzsche through Schopenhauer, Luther writes:

> We are all subjected to the devil with our bodies [. . .] and are foreigners in the world whose prince and god he is. This is why everything is under his control, the bread we eat, the things we drink, the clothes we wear, even the air and everything through which we live in flesh. (quoted in Schopenhauer 2018, ch. 46, p. 596)

Christian writings are not poor in such claims: Jesus instructs his followers to pile up treasures in heaven not on Earth because earthly treasures, unlike their heavenly counterparts, rust, rot and get stolen (Matt 6: 19–21). On Nietzsche's view, this is no accident: 'to talk about "another" world than this is quite pointless' unless we are trying to '*revenge* ourselves on life by means of the phantasmagoria of "another", a "better" life' (*TI* Reason 6; *TI* Untimely 34). As this suggests, he thinks that Christianity invents fictions precisely out of hostility to the real, natural world: 'this entire fictional world has its roots in *hatred* of the natural' (*A* 15). Nietzsche is not condemning the creation of just any non-real world-beyond. One could imagine, and indeed Nietzsche earlier discusses, other kinds of fabricated beyond-worlds, which have the effect of making the real-and-only world seem *better*. Speaking from Hades, Homer's Achilles famously says he would rather be a day-labourer and alive than the king of the underworld and dead – in other words, better to be the worst thing in the everyday world than the best thing in the world-beyond (Odyssey XI, lines 487ff; BT 3). Nietzsche's critical focus, however, rests on those imagined beyond-worlds that assist in the denigration of the world as it really is and of Life's workings within it. Conceiving of heaven helps the Christian to resist the devil on Earth. But that devil, in effect, is the Life Nietzsche wants affirmed, not resisted.

This makes more intuitive the definition of the morality of faithful Christians in terms of (at least apparent) hostility to Life. Ultimately, though, Nietzsche is not exclusively and perhaps not even primarily targeting Christian believers. According to him, at least apparent hostility to Life is the central feature not just of certain kinds of Christianity, but of almost all the moral, religious, political and philosophical standpoints that were immediately available and intuitively appealing to his contemporaries. Nietzsche is not, therefore, making a narrow point about Christianity's ascetic legacy. He is talking about contemporary (nineteenth-century) European values as a whole, or at least in very large part. Christian morality has in some sense *won out* against other moralities, he thinks, and what winning out means is that its status as one among many competitors is no longer visible to us. One might compare this to a struggle between many claimants for the throne of a kingdom. In one, weaker sense, victory would mean seizing the throne from the other claimants. But, in the stronger sense relevant here, victory means seizing the throne and consolidating power in such a way that the other claimants are forgotten and the victor is no longer seen as a 'claimant' *at all*: instead, he is seen as the single and self-evidently legitimate monarch. By all means, various forms of Life-denial might battle it out between them, just as various courtiers might argue about which ceremonial robes the legitimate monarch ought to wear. To get lost in these debates is to miss the bigger picture: all the courtiers agree on who the rightful monarch is, just as all modern outlooks agree on Christian morality, in Nietzsche's sense.

Before we look at various non-Christian versions of Christian morality, note that there are two slightly different claims to be made about their relation to Christianity. The first is that all of these standpoints are (apparently) anti-Life, just as Christian morality is. Understood that way, they are 'Christian', not in any causal or historical sense, but just because they exemplify Christianity's characteristic and peculiar feature, its (at least apparent) hostility to Life. The second is that they are in fact the result of historical, Christian influence. With respect to the outlooks we are about to consider, Nietzsche is always making the first claim and he is often, but not always, making the second. As we shall see, he thinks that both Plato and Kant count as Christian-moral thinkers, but it would be as absurd to suggest that Plato was historically influenced by Christianity as it would be to suggest that Kant was not. Because we will look at Nietzsche's historical account later on, the main focus in this Section will be on the first claim: these outlooks are Christian in the sense that they share its (apparent) hostility to Life.

Note that, to establish this first claim with respect to some outlook, Nietzsche doesn't need to say that it is *explicitly* anti-Life. As it happens, some of the outlooks he considers *are* more or less explicitly anti-Life. But that isn't required. More often, these views oppose some X, where X is a fundamental command, goal or condition of Life. So, if 'Life functions essentially in an injurious, violent, exploitative and destructive manner [...] and it cannot be thought without these characteristics', then, to use Nietzsche's example, being anti-violence and anti-exploitation by forming a legal system that opposes violence and exploitation, would count as being (at least apparently) anti-Life (*GM* II 11). I can be explicitly anti-X and therefore implicitly anti-Life, then, without being *explicitly* anti-Life and without thinking of myself as anti-Life.

There is overlap between these non-Christian 'Christianities', but we can usefully divide them into three categories: philosophy; moral, political and religious outlooks; finally, what I label the 'scholarly outlook'.

2.2 Philosophy as Christian-Moral

In general, Nietzsche treats the history of philosophy as replete with anti-natural or ascetic tendencies, which ally it with Christianity. He calls philosophers 'crypto-priests', emphasising that priestly, Christian ideals have taken hold 'not only within a certain religious community' (*EH* D 2). A first theme is philosophy's hostility to the senses (e.g., *GM* III 7, 28; *TI* 'Reason' 1–2; *GS* 372; see also *GM* I 6 for the equivalent in Christianity). There are two different thoughts here, which are often linked. The first is an epistemic scepticism: according to this tradition, the senses mislead and cannot be trusted. Or, if they do not exactly *mislead*, then they present to us a world that is not the most real, or most significant – a world that is merely apparent, or illusory, or seems to be more important than it really is. Philosophers, therefore, tend to 'demote physicality to the status of illusion' (*GM* III 12). On Nietzsche's account, which refers to and borrows from Schopenhauer, there is a marked tendency, among philosophers, to discover and place high value in a world that (as they see it) is beyond or different from what we erroneously take to be the real world, the latter being the world presented to us by the senses. Indeed, in a passage to which Nietzsche refers in his earlier writings, Schopenhauer claims that a person's capacity for philosophy is indicated by (as Nietzsche summarises it) 'feeling occasionally as if people and all things were mere phantoms or dream-images' (*BT* 1). The positing of a world beyond the senses, one that is more real and more significant than our apparent, sensed world, is recast by Nietzsche as a means to denigrate this world, in which the senses are an important tool for the continuation of life and the furthering of Life's aims. Hence, it is akin to the Christian tool for Life-denial, described in Section 2.1. Here, Nietzsche is thinking of Plato's world of forms, or of the Kantian thing-in-itself, both of which, as he understands them, are fabricated worlds-beyond, created to denigrate this (real and only) world (*TI* Reason 6; *A* 10; *GS* 344; *GM* III 25).

It is likely that Nietzsche has in mind a second kind of hostility – a moral opposition to pleasures that are associated with the senses: food, sex, luxury. Christianity is 'hatred of the senses, of the *joy* of the senses' (*A* 21, my emphasis; also, *GM* III 8) and philosophy generally follows suit. One way into this dual association is to think of words like 'sensuous' or 'sensual', both of which mean *either*, neutrally, 'relating to the senses (as opposed to e.g. the mind)' *or* 'gratifying to the senses', as in a sensual pleasure. A traditional philosophical connection between these two ideas would be that the senses lie about what is real, and therefore that the pleasures associated with them are correspondingly false, or unreal, and indulging them indicates a cognitive failure.

The idea that philosophy is (apparently) anti-Life has another source. Again, we need to look at Schopenhauer and those who followed him. Nietzsche's entire productive life occurred under the aegis of the so-called *Pessimismusstreit* ('pessimism dispute') – the public argument, which began in earnest with Schopenhauer, about whether non-existence was better than existence (for a contemporary analysis, which Nietzsche knew, see Sully 1877; for a modern introduction, see Beiser 2016; on Nietzsche's ethics in relation to the dispute, see Stern 2019b). The 'pessimists', following Schopenhauer, typically argued quite explicitly in favour of non-existence. Nietzsche observed this debate closely, and many of his leading ideas are formulated in response to its participants. That included widely read pessimists like Eduard von Hartmann, Philipp Mainländer and Julius Bahnsen, and optimists like Eugen Dühring, along with many others. Pessimist philosophers like Schopenhauer and Hartmann called, as witnesses, famous authors who (so they claimed) agreed with them. Schopenhauer, for example, claimed that almost all of the 'great minds of every age' have 'recognized the sorrows of this world, and in strong language' (Schopenhauer 2018, ch. 46, p. 601). In addition to Plato, he names philosophers including Heraclitus, Plutarch, Voltaire, Lessing and Hume, along with literary figures including Homer, Sophocles, Euripides, Pliny, Shakespeare, Byron and Leopardi. Hartmann added remarks by Kant and Schelling to the effect that living is worse than being dead (Hartmann 1869, 532–4). Reading all these figures in this way may appear simplified or counterintuitive to the present-day reader. But when Nietzsche writes that 'in every age the wisest have passed the identical judgment on life: *it is worthless*' (*TI* Socrates 1) he is drawing on a (then) not uncommon representation of the history of ideas.

Of course, as we have seen, thinking that it is better to be dead than alive, or that life is miserable, is not the same as opposing Life's goals (in Nietzsche's sense). The distinction between these two was significant at the time. Hartmann argued that we should in fact do what Life (as *he* understood it) orders, just because it is better to be dead than alive: he thought that doing what Life orders us to do was the only way to bring about the final, redemptive end. Mainländer thought that being ascetic *was* what Life (as *he* understood it) really, deeply wanted from us. But, on Nietzsche's understanding of Life, it is generally permissible to infer that someone who espouses the view that the experience of being alive is worthless, miserable and worse-than-nothing is hostile to Life, to the force that produces and governs all biological existence. Moreover, he could reasonably hold that such views were common through the ages.

2.3 Moral, Political and Religious Outlooks as Christian-Moral

As his remarks about Life as appropriation indicated (*BGE* 259, discussed in Section 1), Nietzsche can treat denial of or opposition to one's own interests, preventing the exploitation of others, dominance of the stronger by the weaker, as (at least apparent) hostility to Life. This explains some of Nietzsche's antipathy towards particular moral or political commitments to altruism, egalitarianism, liberalism, socialism and democracy, as well as to some non-Christian religions. We saw that contemporary evolutionary ethics made much of altruism. Schopenhauer spoke of compassion. In both cases, which Nietzsche treats equivalently as versions of the Christian 'love of the neighbour', we see a failure to look out for oneself as one naturally ought to (*TI* Untimely 35–7). What he calls our 'democratic' tendencies are merely a specific instance of a general attempt to deny power, domination and therefore Life (*GM*

II 12; *BGE* 202). Anything that promotes fundamental equality comes in for suspicion, given that Nietzsche sees Life as creating a domain of necessary inequality (*A* 57). The notion of 'equal rights' emerges from Christianity's promotion of the idea that all 'souls' are equal. That idea, of course, is particularly appealing to those who are worse off (*A* 43; also *A* 46; *A* 62). Socialists are agitators who encourage, in workers, the false belief that they are equal (*A* 57; see also *GM* I 5; *GM* II 11); the coming socialist revolution has a similar status to the Christian heaven: designed in opposition to, and from hatred of, the world as it really is (*TI* Untimely 34). In fact, in one note Nietzsche suggests that offering equal rights to those who are not naturally equal, what he calls the 'rejects and rubbish of life', would be 'anti-natural' (*KSA* 13: 23[10]). He concludes: 'it is immoral, it is *anti-natural* in the deepest sense, to say "thou shalt not kill"' (i.e., not kill, or let die, the 'rejects and rubbish of life'). While the unpublished note expresses the point more forcefully and directly, published material is similar (*TI* Untimely 36; *A* 2; *BGE* 62) and we are now in a position to understand how Nietzsche gets to such a position. Life, essentially, is conceived as exploitation and dominance of weaker elements by stronger elements. Hence, protection of the weaker elements is anti-Life. A doctrine of equal rights protects the weak and hence is anti-Life. Although expressed in terms specific to Nietzsche's Life Theory, these ideas reflect Nietzsche's immersion in very common nineteenth-century concerns about the preservation of elements that, supposedly, ought to be dying out (Holub 2018, 408–53).

Nietzsche also treats certain non-Christian religions as anti-Life. In general, he follows Schopenhauer, who identifies some pessimistic elements in Judaism (which Schopenhauer usually takes to be non-pessimistic), as well as in some Eastern religions (Schopenhauer 2018, ch. 46). Of course, Nietzsche need not and does not say that all religions are anti-Life: Ancient Greek and Ancient Israelite religions are not (*GM* II 23; *A* 24–6), and Nietzsche can treat some forms of Eastern religion as superior to Christianity in this respect (*A* 57).

2.4 The Scholarly Outlook as Christian-Moral

Nietzsche, as is often pointed out, was trained as a scholar of antiquity and not as a philosopher. He was given this training at a time and place when it was rigorous, extremely demanding and began at a relatively young age. From quite early on, he had become suspicious of the implicit ideal of this scholarly training, which he took to be that discovering any truth, no matter what, is worth it, no matter the cost. I am calling this ideal the 'scholarly outlook'. That is not exactly Nietzsche's own term: he usually speaks of *Wissenschaft*, which typically translates as 'science'. I prefer to speak of 'the scholarly outlook' because it better reflects what he is getting at: the implicit ideal of scientific and scholarly activity, that no truth is too insignificant, or too elusive, to be worth seeking out, no matter the downsides; that any fact is worth finding out, regardless of the cost (*GS* 344). Nietzsche makes two different claims about this ideal. The first is that it is obviously false: sometimes the truth helps us, sometimes it doesn't. Nietzsche had given various arguments in favour of this conclusion in his earlier writings (*OTL*; *UM* II; *GS* 110–12). More importantly, though – this is the second claim – the premise is *anti-Life*. He claims that Life *requires* error or falsehood, and, hence, that outright opposition to falsehood, like outright opposition to power, exploitation, inequality and so on, equates to an (at least apparent) opposition to Life (*BGE* 4; *BGE* 24; *BT* P 5; *GS* 344; *KSA* 12: 2[119]). The scholarly outlook is therefore a form of Christian morality. Indeed, Nietzsche suggests that the scholar, the one who seeks truth at all costs, is effectively setting up a pretend beyond-world, one in which truth is always good, to slander the real, error-dependent world: the scholarly outlook is Christian in that sense, too (*GS* 344). A Life-denying commitment to truth is, of course, another sense in which *philosophy* is anti-Life, and Nietzsche sometimes suggests that 'we knowers of today', perhaps including Nietzsche, could be accused of being anti-Life in this regard (*GS* 344). Now, it is clearly Nietzsche's view that *Wissenschaft* – science and scholarship – has undermined Christian *faith*, that is, beliefs about the divinity of the historical Jesus, and so on (*GM* III 27). It became harder to believe the sorts of things one was told in church, once one had a nineteenth-century understanding of biological science and critical-historical biblical scholarship. Christianity, as a faith, may therefore encourage opposition to scientific enquiry: Nietzsche reinterprets the story of Adam and Eve in the light of a Judeo-Christian hostility to knowledge (*A* 48–9). But the *significant* feature of Christian morality, for Nietzsche – that it is at least apparently anti-Life – is carried over into the scholarly outlook (*GS* 357).

We are now in a better position to appreciate the scope and significance of Nietzsche's analysis. Of course, many of the positions Nietzsche categorises as instances of Christian morality are not typically thought, by their adherents, to get along very well. Atheist philosophers, socialists, liberals, scholars, Kantians, Platonists, Christians – there may be plenty of overlaps, but there are plenty of disagreements, too. To take one example: Pope Leo XIII, Nietzsche's contemporary, was not overly fond of socialism (see Sommer 2013, 278–9). It is presumably part of the appeal of Nietzsche's analysis that so many different and apparently opposing outlooks can be grouped under one fundamental and negative category.

2.5 Nietzsche's Meta-Ethics

We have now looked at Nietzsche's ethics and at his target, Christian morality. To complete this Section, we can say something about the relationship between them and, consequently, about his meta-ethics, that is, about the status of his claims about ethics and morality. At the start of Section 1, we distinguished between (i) a morality, (ii) Christian morality as an influential instance of a morality and (iii) Nietzsche's ethics. I noted, without explanation, that it would have been misleading to speak of 'Nietzsche's morality' because that would suggest that (iii) his ethical view is just another instance of (i) a morality. On such a (mistaken) view, Nietzsche's ethics and Christian morality would be different species of the same, higher-order kind, just as an apple and an orange are both kinds of fleshy fruit. Nietzsche would be opting for one over the other, according to his own character, preferences or idiosyncrasies, or based on some arguments he provided.

As our analysis shows, though, this is *exactly not* the situation Nietzsche presents in the period we are discussing. His ethics track what he takes to be a deep, fundamental fact about living things, the Life Theory, which applies at all times and in all places. Christian morality is a curious historical phenomenon, a set of values adopted by a particular people at a particular time. Nietzsche thinks that the right way to assess this set of values, Christian morality, or any other morality, is to ask how ethical, how Life-affirming it is – whether its pronouncements accord with the 'aims and objects of Life' (*TI* Morality 6), how it relates to the underlying biological reality (*A* 57). That biological reality makes it impossible to treat everybody equally, so in that sense 'what is right for one' is not 'right for another' (*BGE* 221). But the underlying biological-ethical principle, that Life ought to be affirmed, is held firm at a universal level (*BGE* 221; *A* 11).

If, to the contrary, one takes his ethics as just another instance of a morality, one aids a central misunderstanding of his late position. Something Nietzsche likes to say about *Christian morality* (but not his own ethics) is that its judgements do not touch upon reality at all:

> *there are no moral facts whatever.* Moral judgement has this in common with religious judgement that it believes in realities which do not exist. Morality is merely an interpretation of certain phenomena – more precisely a *mis*interpretation. (*TI* Improvers 1; see also *KSA* 12: 2[165])

If one reads this (wrongly) as saying that Christian morality and *Nietzsche's ethics* – Nietzsche's target for criticism and his preferred alternative – are of the same kind, then one could take Nietzsche's ethics, the command to affirm Life, to have the same relation to reality as Christian morality's judgements. Based on this misunderstanding, Nietzsche's normative command would, by his admission, seem likewise to make no contact with reality. Similarly, one might mistakenly take Nietzsche's opposition to the slogan 'what is right for one is fair for the other' (*BGE* 221) as an opposition to *any* universally applied moral standard, *including* his own ethical standard (cf. Geuss 1997; see Hussain 2013 for various meta-ethical views that have been ascribed to Nietzsche, of which his Section 5.1 offers the closest thing to the correct account for the late works). In fact, as we have seen, Nietzsche's ethical position is (he thinks) firmly based in reality. It is used to measure, 'objectively' (KSA 13: 11 [83]), the status of all moralities, Christian or otherwise – moralities that, physiology aside, have no inherent value (TI Skirmishes 37). Nietzsche's preferred terminology for expressing this way of measuring moralities or sets of values against a deeper, underlying, ethical-natural reality, is that morality is a 'symptom', 'sign-language' or a 'semiotics' (e.g., *TI* Improvers 1; *GM* P 3, 6; III 25; *CW* P; *KSA* 12: 2[165]). The term 'semiotics' had, at the time, a medical connotation: reading the symptoms to reveal a disease (Sommer 2013, 169, 2012, 112–13). It should be noted that Christianity's belief 'in realities which do not exist' is not, itself, an objection. Some moralities are Life-affirming but nonetheless, like Christian morality, they deal in fictions: the Ancient Israelites (before Judaism) and the Ancient Greeks are examples of this. A Life-affirming, Israelite morality might tell its adherents that Yahweh ensures their continuation, power and great destiny (*A* 25). Like Christian morality, Israelite morality believes in realities that do not exist: there is no Yahweh. But Nietzsche's ethical criterion is not 'does this morality posit realities which do not exist?' (an approach that might take him too close to the Life-denying scholarly outlook) but rather: 'are these values Life-affirming?' In this case they are because they reveal a '*correct*, that is to say, natural relation to all things' (*A* 25). So, the symptoms (a morality) reveal something about Life. The question for the next part of our discussion is: What exactly does Christian morality reveal about Life?

Before looking at answers to this question, two last points. First, we have said that, in addition to claiming that Christian morality is unethical, Nietzsche *also* claims that what is *ethical* is Christian-*immoral*. These mutual condemnations are asymmetrical. By analogy, finding ethics immoral is like finding the laws of physics immoral, whereas finding Christian morality unethical is a bit like finding Christian morality contrary to the laws of physics. If you plan a building that would contravene the laws of physics, then that's your problem; if you disapprove of the laws of physics, well, that's your problem, too. We are about to see that Nietzsche cannot argue in quite such a simple way. But the analogy is intended to emphasise, once more, that he does not present his ethics and Christian morality simply as equivalent and rival modes of evaluation. Second, there is an important, but completely different, meta-ethical question about the status of Nietzsche's *ethical* claim that Life's goals ought to be furthered. We address this in Section 6.3.

3 The Square Circle: Nietzsche's Two Conflicting Strategies

This study aims to aid the reader's understanding of Nietzsche and to set the record straight about the ethics of his late works. In Nietzsche's particular case, however, the best way to *explain* his ideas is to show how he is employing two different strategies as part of his opposition to Christian morality and, importantly, to show that these strategies *conflict*. My purpose in highlighting the conflict is not to attack or refute Nietzsche's position as a whole. Apart from anything else, that seems redundant because the reader probably does not hold the Life Theory upon which Nietzsche builds his ethics. (We discuss Nietzschean ethics without the Life Theory in the conclusion.) Examining these two strategies, and the conflict between them, is the best way to understand what Nietzsche is doing and why he is doing it – that includes why he can say different, conflicting things about Life, ethics and morality. What I am offering, therefore, is exegesis in the form of internal criticism. One would be tempted to call the tension between his two strategies a prism through which to view Nietzsche's late work, but, given its self-conflicting nature, I'll refer to it as the 'square circle'. In this section, the square circle is constructed. In the next section, we look through the square circle at the best known of Nietzsche's late writings on morality.

Earlier, I advertised the peculiar phrasing chosen to describe Christian morality's attitude to Life: that it is *at least apparently* anti-Life. As explained, the wording remained neutral between two different claims that Nietzsche might be making. (i) Christian morality successfully prevents Life from achieving its goals. (ii) Christian morality merely makes claims or utters slogans that advocate preventing Life from achieving its goals, or it merely presents behaviours that *appear, misleadingly, at first sight* to impede Life – but it does not in fact impede Life. Following (ii), for example, the Christian might say things like 'power seeking is evil and ought to be opposed!', while *behaving* in a way that is *not* anti-Life, like seeking out power; indeed, the Christian might even seek power *by* uttering slogans like 'oppose all power seeking!'.

It is now time to explore how these different senses in which Christian morality might be called 'anti-Life' – (i) genuinely inhibiting Life, or (ii) merely uttering anti-Life slogans (etc.) as part of a Life-promoting tactic – are at play in Nietzsche's two anti-Christian strategies. It will be helpful to have labels for Nietzsche's two strategies, which I present, initially, as arguments abstracted from the texts. I will call them the 'Unethical Strategy', which is based on (i), and the 'Impossible Strategy', based on (ii). The Unethical Strategy claims that

Christian morality really impedes Life's goals, and hence is *unethical*. The Impossible Strategy claims that Christianity by all means produces anti-Life slogans and apparently anti-Life behaviours, but does *not* impede Life's goals because impeding Life's goals is *impossible*.

The Unethical Strategy: an argument to establish that Christian morality (and therefore more or less the entirety of contemporary European morality) is unethical.

U1: The central and defining feature of Christian morality is that it prevents Life from achieving its goals.

U2: More or less the entirety of contemporary European morality is Christian in this sense.

U3: To prevent Life from achieving its goals just is to be *unethical*.

U4: Therefore, more or less the entirety of contemporary European morality is *unethical*.

The Impossible Strategy: an argument to establish that one cannot really impede Life's goals.

I1: The central and defining feature of Christian morality is that it utters anti-Life slogans or *prima facie* appears to be anti-Life.

I2: More or less the entirety of contemporary European morality is Christian in this sense.

I3: No living thing can prevent Life from achieving its goals: uttering anti-Life slogans or appearing to be anti-Life *always* conceals a strategy on Life's part to achieve its goals as best it can.

I4: Therefore, more or less the entirety of contemporary European morality conceals an operation on behalf of Life: it does not successfully hinder Life, but rather helps Life achieve its goals.

The Unethical Strategy is, in essence, what we have presented so far: Christianity really impedes Life. This strategy is the driving force behind Nietzsche's ethics. But the Impossible Strategy is also present, and for a good reason, even if (I shall claim) it ought probably to be assigned a subordinate role. These strategies do not get along. Start with the claim that preventing Life from achieving its goals is unethical (U3) and add it, as a premise, to the Impossible Strategy's argument. It is consistent, but it yields a further conclusion:

IU: Nothing living is unethical.

We can call this 'IU' because it combines both strategies (it is Impossible to be Unethical). However: if nothing living is unethical (if IU is true), then real, living Christians are not unethical (U4 is false). Nietzsche would most likely prefer to reject IU and keep U4. His *whole point* appears to be that Christian morality inhibits Life (i.e., is unethical), whereas IU produces an ethical principle from which one cannot possibly stray – a problem Nietzsche remarks on, when criticising a different account of natural ethics (*BGE* 9).

Nietzsche's best option, then, would likely be to reject the claim that Life always operates *to its maximal advantage* through living beings. Life is always operating, but not always operating as best it could. This denies I3 and therefore I4. The Unethical Strategy remains in place and the Impossible Strategy is suitably modified so that it no longer clashes with its neighbour.

This option, I think, neatly summarises a move Nietzsche very often makes. But, here, I want to emphasise two points. First, it is not *always* the move he makes – the Impossible Strategy is really present in the late works. Second, and more importantly, the Impossible Strategy is there *for a reason*. It is the Impossible Strategy that enables Nietzsche to turn to Christian-moral opponents, and to tell them that they are advocating something *impossible* (e.g., equality within an organic realm that is governed by anti-egalitarian Life) and not merely something *possible but bad*. Were Nietzsche to admit that impeding Life's goals is a living possibility, then the egalitarian could respond: 'Well, you admit it is perfectly possible to treat people equally and to stay alive! You say that exploitation "belongs to the *essence* of what lives". If you mean, by that, that I cannot stay alive without exploiting, then you are wrong by your own admission. If you mean that I *ought* not to stay alive without exploiting, then you have given me no reasons to agree. I don't like the sound of this "Life" character, and I'll do what I can to impede it.' The Impossible Strategy, in reply, tells the egalitarian that, to the contrary, she or he certainly is being exploitative: all living things exploit; an organism that does not exploit will die off (*BGE* 259). Without the Impossible Strategy, he admits that genuine, Christian morality is possible, if bad, and then he has to say *why* it is bad. As we shall see, Nietzsche does not have a good answer to this (Section 6.3).

For the moment, with both strategies in mind, we can understand what Nietzsche is doing when he makes differing claims and why there is a tension between them. Take, for example, his account of the philosopher's characteristic antipathy for sensuality (Section 2.1) – here, sex and marriage. Nietzsche's point, in what follows, is that this antipathy is not *real* hostility to Life, because it *cannot* be:

> Every animal, including the *bête philosophe*, instinctively strives for an optimum of favourable conditions in which to fully release his power and achieve his maximum of power-sensation; every animal abhors equally instinctively [...] any kind of disturbance and hindrance that blocks or could block his path to the optimum [i.e., 'the path to power']. Thus the

> philosopher abhors *marriage*, together with all that might persuade him to it.
> (*GM* III 7)

Nietzsche concludes that such a philosopher affirms Life. This accords with his general understanding of affirmation as doing what Life wants, seeking power. It follows the Impossible Strategy. *Apparent* anti-Life behaviour (here, the philosopher's hostility to sex and reproduction) is not *real* anti-Life behaviour because it *can't* be – in fact, it is just another instance of power-maximising behaviour (see also *KSA* 13: 11[96]; 14[75]; 14[140]; 14[182]). The same is true of the priest: just like every other animal, he acts to maximise power in Nietzsche's sense. Even as he describes the Jewish priests seizing power in *A*, and explicitly calls their *values* anti-natural, he also says that Life is working through them to make them 'stronger' than the rest: 'this kind of man has a Life-interest in making mankind *sick* and in inventing the concepts "good" and "evil", "true" and "false" in a mortally dangerous and world-defaming sense' (*A* 24, translation altered; also *EH* Destiny 7). To read this, one could gather that philosophers and priests are doing what they are sup-posed to do, or at least that Life is doing what it is supposed to do (and necessarily does) through them. To be sure, their official *utterances* are world defaming and Life-denying, but their *behaviour* – seeking power to the maximum of their ability – is perfectly natural and affirmative in furthering Life's goals.

Yet, if the Impossible Strategy is taken as seriously as these passages suggest, then Nietzsche's project is threatened by Nietzsche's own standards: apparently anti-natural philosophers and priests would be maximising power like any other creature and *therefore not doing anything unethical* (IU).

It is instructive to compare the above remarks about the priest (within the Impossible Strategy) with the following:

> Every kind of anti-nature is a vice. The most vicious kind of man is the priest: he teaches anti-nature. [...] The preaching of sexual modesty is a public incitement to anti-nature. Every condemnation of sexual life, every soiling of sexual life with the concept of 'impurity' is the real sin against the holy spirit of Life. (*A*, 'Law against Christianity' [*KSA* 6, p. 254, my translation])

In presenting us with living instances of genuine, anti-natural activity, such claims reject the Impossible Strategy's central line. Likewise, to sum-marise *EH* D 2: a degenerate (anti-natural) part of an organism threatens to ruin the whole and ought to be cut out; the priest, however, asks us to sympathise with the degenerate part; therefore, he '*conserves* what degen-erates'. This is the attitude that enables Nietzsche to hope for a 'new party of Life which would tackle the greatest of all tasks, the attempt to raise humanity higher, including the relentless destruction of everything that was degenerating and parasitical' (*EH* BT 4), where priests are often described as parasites (*A* 26, *A* 38, *A* 49) who desire 'the degeneration of the whole' (*EH* D 2).

Are philosopher-priests unethical Life-impeders, dangerous and in need of destruction? Or are they just another instance of Life promoting itself as best it can? Are they driven by the 'ulterior motive of revenging themselves against Life' (*EH* Destiny 7) or (in the very same aphorism) do they merely use Christian morality as 'the means to come to *power*'? We need not chose, only understand why he says each: the claim that anti-sensual philosophers and priests are maximally Life-driven is part of the Impossible Strategy, whereas hostile condemnation of parasitical, Life-impeding priests is part of the Unethical Strategy.

The square circle helps in another, important respect. It explains the difficulty of pinning Nietzsche down on which specific activities *really are* ethical or unethical, that is, what Life really wants from us. We might have thought that outright hostility to sexuality would be a clear-cut case: if *anything* is anti-natural, it ought to be *that*. Yet, as we have seen, Nietzsche also says, and is motivated to say, that philosophers' anti-sexuality is *not anti-natural*: Life is still omnipotently directing the proceedings, and so must have an interest in making people avoid sex or even in making them loudly condemn it (GM III 7–10). Getting too bogged down in which kinds of behaviours, or even which kinds of behaviours in which kinds of people and under which circumstances, count as unethical for Nietzsche is to miss the wood for the trees. The Impossible Strategy operates precisely to show that *any* instance of *any* behaviour displays Life making its best effort to promote its goals, while the Unethical Strategy opposes exactly that view.

To repeat, my aim is not to present the square circle as a watertight objection to Nietzsche, let alone to a philosophical interpreter arguing on his behalf, who willingly overlooks certain passages and creatively reinterprets others. My aim is exegetical. This is a tension in Nietzsche's writing, and understanding it helps to understand him. As I have already suggested, Nietzsche's writings offer one prominent attempt to confront the square circle by abandoning the Impossible Strategy: all things are indeed Life-y to some extent, so this attempt goes, but some things are Life-ier than others, and we ought to make everything maximally Life-y. I have already mentioned the challenge facing this line: Nietzsche then has to say *why* we ought to further Life's goals and, I will suggest, he has no good answer. We will come to that soon enough (Section 6.3). For the moment, we need only look through the square circle onto Nietzsche's best-known text.

4 Morality, History and Genealogy

Nietzsche's writings on Christian morality are notable because, in some significant cases, they take the form of *histories*. In the period we are examining, Nietzsche wrote two histories, *GM* and *A*, that agree in outline though they differ in their details, emphasis and scope. There are also briefer historical sketches in other books of the period (e.g., *TI* Socrates). We will primarily look at *GM*'s historical narrative, using other late works to supplement our understanding.

We can helpfully begin by asking the question: Given his ethics, why would Nietzsche feel inclined to write a history of Christian morality? Three main goals stand out. The first is to persuade the reader that Life really does work as he claims it does. We have seen that his Life Theory, and the normative command he builds on it, would not have seemed as alien then as now. But it does not follow – nor is it true – that everybody would have agreed with him. His historical account will try to persuade them. This goal is pursued in two ways. First, the reader will see Life operating in different beings, at different times and places. Life's operations, and Life's versatility, will be put on display: we will see Life in action. The second way this motivation plays out is subtler. Nietzsche holds that Christian morality has mediated our understanding of Life. Not only is Christianity at least apparently anti-natural, and not only do we not really understand how Life works: Christianity has *clouded* our understanding of Life's nature and functioning (*A* 15). So, for example, Nietzsche thinks that the notion of free will is *both* false to nature, that is, not a good description of how we act, *and* anti-natural, that is, a theory invented to serve (at least apparently) anti-natural, Christian purposes. Nietzsche's histories will show this, too. I will refer to this function of Nietzsche's histories as showing 'obfuscation in action', that is, demonstrating how Christian morality systematically misleads us about how Life works. Nietzsche, as we have seen, is adamant that *some* errors are necessary for Life (Section 2.4), so the objection cannot be to error or obfuscation as such, but rather to obfuscation about Life, insofar as it prevents us from affirming Life.

Suppose you have been persuaded that Life functions as Nietzsche claims it does. Now, a different question comes into view, which motivates the second aim of the histories. In *GS* 344, Nietzsche describes the following as the 'moral problem': '*why morality at all,* if Life, nature and history are "immoral" ["*unmoralisch*"]?' To translate this into the terms I have been using, the question is this: Why did Christian morality succeed, flourish and dominate, given that it seems in direct opposition to how Life operates? How did we moderns end up with an (apparently) anti-Life morality? Consider, similarly, the following questions from a late note: 'Why did Life, physiological well-constitutedness everywhere succumb? Why was there no philosophy of Yes, religion of Yes? [...] Is man therefore an exception in the history of Life?' (*KSA* 13: 14[137]). Again, the point of these questions is clear: Life guarantees, or ought to guarantee, a philosophy and a religion of Yes, of Life-affirmation, of doing what Life instructs, wants or programmes. Why do we moderns appear to be different?

A history of morality will answer this question. It will explain how we ended up where we are, despite or because of a Life-governed world. But it is here that Nietzsche's investigation is guided (and confused) by the square circle, by the attempt to show that anti-Life morality is unethical and impossible. For *just what is it* that the history will show? Will the narrative adopt the Unethical Strategy, showing that we *are* 'an exception in the history of life'? Or will Nietzsche claim that we are *not* an exception, following the Impossible Strategy? *GM* begins by implying the Unethical claim, at least as a rhetorical question: what if 'morality itself were to blame if man, as species, never reached his highest power and splendour?' (*GM* P 6). The suggestion, understandably, is that anti-natural morality impedes Life, so that Life fails to achieve what it might. But the text is also driven by the Impossible Strategy, by the desire to show us that Life is always and everywhere maximally in force (*GM* III 7), thus rendering futile Christian morality's resistance to it.

It seems plausible that Nietzsche has a third goal in mind, namely to persuade his reader to be more ethical, natural and Life-affirming (see e.g., *GM* II 24's 'reverse experiment'). As *GM* P 6 suggests, he sometimes has it that anti-natural morality has impeded Life, and from that perspective it would make sense to motivate readers to aid Life's struggle. Christianity, as we shall see, arose from what Nietzsche calls a 'revaluation of values' (*TI* Improvers 4; *GM* I 7–8), when values switched from being natural to being (at least apparently) anti-natural. A looser, but nonetheless helpful translation of this phrase would be a 'turnaround in values': Nietzsche presents himself as heralding another revaluation, a turning-back-around, a re-turn to natural values (*A* 61; *EH* Clever 9; *EH GM*). But this only makes sense in light of the Unethical Strategy. It makes no sense at all as part of the Impossible Strategy, the central claim of which is that we are, always, maximally Life-driven: there could be nothing to persuade us to do.

In sum, we might distinguish three aims at work in Nietzsche's historical writing:

1. Persuade the reader that Life works as Nietzsche claims, by a) showing Life in action and b) showing obfuscation in action.

2. For the reader who sees how Life works, answer the pressing question: So how did we end up with an anti-Life morality?

3. Persuade the reader to abandon an anti-Life morality in favour of a Life-affirming one.

In some ways, these goals can be mutually reinforcing. Take the two parts of the first motivation: because we misunderstand Life, it is easier to hold anti-natural views; but anti-natural views, in turn, encourage a misunderstanding of Life. Showing obfuscation in action explains and clears away various misunderstandings about Life, which in turn enables the reader to accept the descriptions of Life in action. The Christian might come to think: 'Christian morality implanted in me the false belief that I had free will. This belief prevented me from understanding, as I now do, how Life really works.' Not only that, but the two parts can combine: Christianity's obfuscation might be Life-governed, so showing obfuscation in action is often enough *also* a matter of showing Life in action. The Christian might come to think: 'The vehemence of my attachment to free will arose from Christianity's apparent hostility to nature [obfuscation in action], but this apparent hostility to nature was Life's plan all along! [Life in action].' The second goal is to answer a question made pressing when the reader has the right understanding of Life, which can be brought about by the first: 'yes', the Christian might ask, 'why *do* I oppose power seeking, expansion and exploitation, when that is the essence of living beings like me?' Nietzsche may expect this, in turn, to make the third motivation more likely to succeed (the Christian might say: 'nothing now prevents me from acting in a Life-affirming manner!'). But these aims can also conflict. If showing Life in action means showing Life always, omnipotently in action (the Impossible Strategy), then – as we saw – there is no room to persuade someone to be more ethical and the third aim is thereby thwarted.

Before we look in more detail at how Nietzsche attempts to achieve his aims, one more comment on genealogy is required. One welcome impact of Nietzsche's work is the philosophical legacy of a genealogical method (Foucault 1977; Geuss 1999, 2002; Williams 2002). There is plenty of disagreement about what 'genealogy' means in its own right: it is an ambiguous term and of course the waters are muddied by different interpretations of Nietzsche. The question of whether something by the name of 'genealogy' is philosophically fruitful stands apart from the question of what Nietzsche was doing and we are concerned, here, exclusively with the latter. In that regard, note that *GM* does not present genealogy as a stand-alone *method*, and that *A*, although evidently a history of a somewhat similar kind, does not call itself a 'genealogy'. Moreover, *GM* by no means presents its author as the *only* or the *first* moral genealogist, but rather as the best one. There have been other moral genealogists, *GM* says, but Nietzsche is best because his approach to history is not governed by Christian morality and, relatedly, his view of Life is not obfuscated. That means, for example, that he does not unthinkingly seek to glorify or justify Christian morality; he does not see its progress as inevitable or welcome; and he does not treat Christian morality as universal and unconditionally binding. If so, *GM* can justifiably claim to present a less biased history.

However, one thing we have remarked on, and will see in full force as we look at the texts, is that Nietzsche's history-writing presupposes the Life Theory. The Life Theory is present in each of the aims we just set out, but most importantly in the first one: it governs the way Nietzsche thinks about, analyses and presents historical phenomena, because these phenomena, in the end, have some relation to Life's operations (*BGE* 259; *GM* II 12). It is an obvious question for us to ask whether, and how, a genealogy of the kind that Nietzsche writes could function without his particular and, we might now think, peculiar Life Theory. But one of the intriguing and frustrating things about real, historical figures is that they very often do not see a distinction exactly where, to us, a distinction is obvious and important. Nietzsche never wrote a genealogy without presupposing the Life Theory and the ethics he builds upon it, so genealogy and the Life Theory are intertwined in *GM*: pulling them apart will not leave Nietzsche's project, itself, intact. This remark is by no means intended to discourage the use of genealogy in philosophy, understood in various ways. The point, rather, is to make it clear where Nietzsche-interpretation ends and where something else begins.

5 Nietzsche's History: The Plot

With Nietzsche's aims in mind, this section turns to the history, using *GM* as the backbone, and adding material from *A*. I have already given away the ending of the story: the triumph of Christian morality, of (apparent) hostility to Life. Once we have a better view of the history, we turn to the question of whether the history achieves its aims (Section 6).

5.1 *GM* I: Good, Bad and Evil

The first essay argues that there is a distinction between two kinds of morality: master morality and slave morality. There are historical instances of both, but we can think of them as general types. Master morality has it that what masters approve of is good. Slave morality says that what slaves approve of is good. Master morality is prior; a slave revolt in morals follows; we Europeans now have, overwhelmingly, a slave morality.

The historical difference and struggle between master morality and slave morality can be observed, Nietzsche thinks, in our everyday language and in the etymology of our words. He starts with an observation about our everyday language – he means German, of course, but English is similar in this respect. The term 'good' has two opposites: 'bad' and 'evil'. The good that pairs with bad is different from the good that pairs with evil. But it is not an accident that the same word, 'good', means two different things. The good of the pair good-vs.-bad, call it 'good (vs. bad)', is associated with the master morality. The other good, call it 'good (vs. evil)', is associated with the slave morality. Before we get to Nietzsche's specific claims, we can see from our own use how the two goods (and their opposites) look different. When you say that your dog has been a 'good dog', or when you say that the train is a 'good way to get to the airport', you are evaluating these things. In each case, the opposite evaluation would be to say that they are 'bad'. Still, you aren't evaluating them *morally* as you would now understand that term. Certainly, you wouldn't think they were evil. When it comes to people, though, and we say that someone is good, or that an action is good, then 'evil' becomes a more appropriate opposite term. The opposite of a good action is, or could be, evil, but the same is not true for a good train.

On Nietzsche's telling, the masters are wealthier and more powerful (*GM* I 5). They are healthier, having better access to material resources. The slaves are the opposite: poorer, weaker and sicker. Nietzsche asks: Which values would be expressed by these different groups? For the masters, being good would mean being like them: healthy, wealthy, powerful, while those who are not good in this sense would be bad. Nietzsche offers etymological arguments for his historical claims: words for *good* in Greek, Latin and German tend, so he says, to be associated with power, the trappings of power (wealth), or with specific moral or physical characteristics of the powerful group in question (truthful; blond and light-skinned) (*GM* I 4–5). The words for *bad*, meanwhile, are often associated with what is, in a neutral sense, plain or ordinary, before then becoming associated, in a pejorative sense, with what is bad: in English, think of words like 'simple', 'plain', 'common' or 'ordinary', which have both neutral and pejorative meanings.

There are two important characteristics to note about the masters' mode of evaluation because they differ markedly, in these respects, from slave morality and, therefore, from Christian morality. First, Nietzsche seems to take it that an important kind of superiority of the masters is fairly self-evident to all parties, perhaps including the reader (*GM* I 10). The masters don't need a theory explaining why it is better to be healthy, rich or powerful. Second, the verdict that masters deliver on slaves lacks some of the characteristics of Christian morality. For one thing, the masters do not say that it is the *fault* of the slaves that they are bad. Being enslaved might be a matter of being in the wrong place at the wrong time. Of course, it is *bad* to be a slave, and the life of the slave is worse than that of the master. But the master does not need a special story about what a slave did wrong to make him end up a slave. Moreover, being bad doesn't mean being selfish or violent – two Christian-moral vices. The slaves might well be selfish and violent, as might the masters, or they might be pacific and selfless. Either way, they are bad. This doesn't mean that they are hated by the masters, and they may even be the objects of a certain patronising, benevolent affection (*GM* I 10).

What Nietzsche calls the 'slaves' revolt in morality' (*GM* I 7) occurs when the term 'evil' is invented to refer to the same set of characteristics that the masters had grouped under the label 'good': in other words, after the revolt, it becomes evil to be wealthy, powerful and healthy. The *label*, 'good', is retained but now attached to those things that were previously considered to be bad, that is, being a slave, being poor, unhealthy, disempowered. Whereas the masters look to themselves, label themselves 'good', and then call slaves 'bad', the slaves are driven by resentment of their masters (Nietzsche uses the French word, *ressentiment*), call masters 'evil' and, therefore, themselves 'good' (*GM* I 10–11).

Nietzsche claims that the '*slaves' revolt in morality* begins with the Jews: a revolt which has two thousand years of history behind it' (*GM* I 7). Nietzsche's views on Jews and Judaism are complex and contested (Holub 2016). The mention of 'two thousand years', and the opposition of the Jews to the Romans, suggests that, in *GM*, he has in mind Jews living under Roman domination (*GM* I 16), whom, as he claims in *BGE* 195, Tacitus calls 'born for slavery' (although Nietzsche likely has Cicero, not Tacitus, in mind: see Sommer 2016, 527–8). In *A* 24–6, however, Nietzsche looks back earlier, and more plausibly, to the defeat of the two proto-Jewish kingdoms of Israel and Judah, and to the theological responses to those defeats that presaged a new conception of Yahweh and of morality (Stern 2019a). Generally, there is some confusion in Nietzsche's writings about whether he takes this revolt to be something that the slaves organise (*BGE* 260) or whether it is directed by sickly but *noble* priests, who are at odds with other, warrior-like nobles (*GM* I 6–7) or who act opportunistically in the light of the nobles' military defeat (*A* 24–6). A related suggestion is that the Jews, taken as a whole, function as an oppressed but 'priestly people' or 'priestly nation' (*GM* I 7, 16), with the historical Jesus as the representative of the 'slaves' *within* that priestly nation (*A* 27). Whichever historical group he has in mind, Nietzsche also sees the Jews as exemplifying – that is, both being a typical example of, and being an impressive or unusually powerful example of – a trend that can be found throughout history to some degree (*GM* I 16). Moreover, his general point is that contemporary, Christian morality owes a great deal to the Jewish revolt – a fact that he thinks will be uncomfortable to some anti-Jewish readers (*A* 24, 27). Here, he summarises the line taken by 'the Jews', which characterises the slaves' revolt:

> Only those who suffer are good, only the poor, the powerless, the lowly are good; the suffering, the deprived, the sick, the ugly are the only pious people, the only ones saved, salvation is for them alone, whereas you rich, the noble and the powerful, you are eternally wicked, cruel, lustful, insatiate, godless [. . .] (*GM* I 7)

At first glance, it might seem as though, with the slave revolt, we have a simple swap: 'good' labels what was formerly considered bad (slaves), 'evil' labels what was formerly considered 'good' (masters). But recall that, in contrast to the term 'bad', only *people and their actions* are called 'evil'. And recall that good (vs. bad) does not imply praise for any particular actions. Nietzsche thinks he can explain this change using the slave revolt. We saw that the masters do not need to work very hard to convince themselves that they are better off than the slaves. But the slaves, if they want to say that they are good, *do* need to explain why goodness, as common sense might have it, is not attached to material well-being or power. Nietzsche claims that this is where the idea of 'free will' comes in – in fact, this is the purpose for which it is invented.

Free will is a good example of obfuscation in action. Nietzsche thinks it is an idiosyncrasy of the language group he is considering – roughly, the Indo-Germanic group including 'Indian, Greek and German' languages (*BGE* 20; also *BGE* 17) – that describing an event obliges us to divide the event between subject and verb, even when there is obviously something artificial about this division. We say, for example, that 'lightning strikes'. But we are really describing only one thing. It is not as though there is lightning, waiting up there in the sky, prior to its striking. Grammatically, of course, we could say that the lightning ran or evaporated or prevaricated. But, of course, it struck because the lightning *is* the striking. You would struggle to say that there is some lightning, without doubling it, without putting together a subject and a verb: 'Lightning!' 'Lightning-is-happening!' This accident of language makes it easier to think of the lightning as set apart from its flashing or striking, as a kind of *subject* lying behind or beyond that flashing: 'the common people separates lightning from its flash and takes the latter to be a *deed*, something performed by a subject, which is called lightning' (*GM* I 13). It is similar with claims about people. I say, 'I opened the door', and it is easy to imagine an 'I' apart from the opening of the door. Really, as with lightning, there is only one thing or event: a me-opening-the-door. Hence, it becomes easier to imagine that the 'I' in question might really have done something else, like writing a letter. Here, linguistically and therefore conceptually, the space for a free entity, a free will, is created. I can be thought to be behind or beyond any particular action and, just a short conceptual move from there, I can be supposed to be free to perform or refrain from any given action. Those who speak such a language will find it easier to maintain, to themselves and others, that there is, as Nietzsche puts it, a '"being" behind the deed' (*GM* I 13).

This is then applied to the masters: if all of us have chosen what we do and are, then the masters were free to be slaves, but chose not to be, and the slaves are free to be masters, but choose not to be. This has obvious advantages for the slaves' outlook. Masters are not just luckier than slaves: luck doesn't really come into it. Some people choose to be evil, and behave in a masterly way, whereas others choose to be good and behave as the slaves do. The slaves now have a flattering story about why they are as they are. Nietzsche illustrates this by imagining a confrontation between birds of prey (masters) and their prey, lambs (slaves), noting the differences in how each thinks about the other. Birds of prey do not *hate* lambs: there is nothing tastier than a nice lamb. But nor do they wish to be like lambs. Lambs, of course, *do* hate the birds of prey that threaten to snatch them away and destroy them. Nietzsche likens slaves, who attribute free will to their masters by saying that masters could have acted otherwise, to lambs who criticise birds of prey for not nibbling grass like a lamb, or, equivalently, to lambs who tell themselves that they could have been birds of prey and deserve praise for not being so (*GM* I 13).

It looks likely from his discussion of free will that Nietzsche thinks the slaves' claim is false: masters cannot choose, out of their own free will, to act as slaves. Certainly, Nietzsche remained a trenchant critic of free will, understood in this way (Forster 2019). However, if his implication is that there are deeds without subjects, then that is at least a difficult claim to get along with, philosophically and exegetically (Pippin 2006). Our focus is not on Nietzsche's purported underlying theory of action or will, which would require its own treatment (for discussion, see Stern 2015). We are concentrating, instead, on his account of the origin and function of the Christian theory of free will, a theory that Nietzsche takes to be false. As *GM* I 13 makes clear, the concept has an obfuscatory function, impeding the correct understanding of how Life works, how strength inevitably expresses itself, as 'a desire to overthrow, crush, become master [...]. A quantum of force is just such a quantum of drive, will, action, in fact it is nothing but this driving, willing and acting [...].' The powerful will do as they wish, Nietzsche appears to say, and the weak will suffer what they must. This all sounds very familiar from the earlier discussions of Life, only now we have seen the motivations for obfuscation. It is in the slaves' interests not to understand how Life works, that is, how strength always expresses itself. But before we leave things there, we might pause for a moment over Nietzsche's chosen illustration: lambs (a recognisable symbol of Judeo-Christian morality) and the birds of prey, presumably eagles (a symbol of Rome), who fly down and snatch them away. One contrast Nietzsche has in mind here is that between the Romans, as 'masters', and the Jews (and, later, also Christians) under their rule, as 'slaves'. If so, his animal examples are carefully chosen: For what eventually happens to these particular birds of prey, the Romans? The answer is that they *become lambs*, converting, in the end, to Christianity. Nietzsche has indeed already subtly referenced the conversion of Constantine the Great, who became the first Christian emperor (*GM* I 8). It may be ridiculous to expect birds of prey to become lambs, but, given time, that is exactly what happened. This does not mean, of course, that the Christian theory of free will is correct. But it does press the question: *How* did it happen? In a sense, that is the question Nietzsche is trying to answer, as per the second aim (Section 4). We shall return to how he answers it (see Section 6.2). Meanwhile, free will is not *GM* I's only example of obfuscation in action. One passage notes that contemporary Christian-moral people have come to see themselves as 'the aim and pinnacle, the meaning of history' (*GM* I 11). Of course, if you see the promotion of Christian morality as the meaning of history, then you will not be able to grasp that Life, not an (apparently) anti-Life morality, is history's guiding force. We will say more about obfuscation in Christian historiography when discussing *GM* II (Sections 5.2 and 7.1).

We have said that Nietzsche analyses moralities as signs or symptoms, reading off them whether their adherents affirm or (at least apparently) obstruct Life. One might expect master and slave moralities to fit neatly into these respective categories. Masters are powerful, aware of this power, act on it and affirm its importance. They certainly look Life-affirming enough. Nietzsche says as much: in a later remark about *GM* I, he describes the masters' morality as natural and Life-affirming, in contrast to the slaves' morality (*A* 24). Or again: master morality 'is the sign-language of what has turned out well, of *ascending* life, of the will to power as the principle of life. Master morality *affirms* as instinctively as Christian morality *negates*' (*CW*, Epilogue). But matters are not quite so simple. For example, Nietzsche has some grudgingly positive things to say about the slave revolt: the priests are intelligent and they make, of man, an 'interesting animal' (*GM* I 6–7, 10), although being interesting does not entail being Life-affirming. Generally, Nietzsche's attitude to slave morality is confused by the square circle. For what should we make of those responsible for the slave revolt, such as these clever priests? Are they being genuinely anti-natural, unethical, but therefore unlike all other living things and a challenge to

Nietzsche's description of Life? Or, are they acting as all living things do, but therefore *not* being unethical? After all, they are seeking power.

5.2 *GM* II: Moral Conscience

What we saw in the first essay was a social description of why certain values might come in handy. Believing that they are good, and that they have chosen to be as they are, is helpful for the slaves. But those who adhere to Christian morality do not, of course, *think* that they are doing so for prudential reasons. To the contrary, they think that they are *right* about what is good and what is evil. One reason why they think they are right is that they consider themselves to have access to a kind of moral knowledge: for example, in *Genesis*, Adam and Eve gain the knowledge of good and evil. One way this knowledge might be taken to express itself is through their conscience, which seems to let them know when they do evil things.

Nietzsche need not deny that our moral intuitions accord with Christian morality, nor that we have an *apparent*, intuitive knowledge of what is good and what is evil. But the story of the first essay has already to some degree raised a question mark about this apparent knowledge. Nietzsche's masters did not feel guilty when performing the same sorts of actions that we, now, would feel guilty for performing. This, in itself, cannot settle things: the Christian can say, as some of the moral historians Nietzsche was reading did say, that earlier peoples were simply less moral than we are (see Lecky 1921, 1:99–102, which Nietzsche read in translation). When we meet people, now, who do not appear to have a conscience, we do not try to learn from them or take them to refute our moral views. One way into the second essay of the *Genealogy* is to think of it as Nietzsche's attempt to explain feelings of conscience, guilt and regret, without according them any status as moral knowledge. His explanation is inventive and speculative, involving the confluence of three different factors, none of which, initially, has anything to do with moral knowledge.

Nietzsche's first claim is that pain makes us remember things (*GM* II 3). Think of a particular kind of food you ate, which made you vomit. You probably don't want to eat it again. In the background of his claim about pain and memory is a further idea of his: memory-formation is extremely difficult for human beings because we are working all the time to *forget* information that would otherwise weigh us down (on the weight of the past, see his earlier essay, *UM* II). Humans are not really set up for memory-acquisition unless, as in painful cases, there is an obvious payoff, like not being violently ill. Pain, then, is a way of getting past our actively forgetful defences. As *GM* II 3 makes clear, this includes witnessing the pain of *others*.

Second, quite independently of the previous story, pain has another role in our early history, which involves the relation between creditors and debtors. We can take a well-known example from the literature Nietzsche was drawing on (Kohler 1885, 19–20; on Kohler's influence, see Sommer 2019, esp. 268–9). In *The Merchant of Venice*, Antonio borrows three thousand ducats from Shylock. Antonio promises to pay back the loan when his ships arrive. But if, for some reason, the ships never make it, then what guarantee can Antonio offer to Shylock instead of the money? The answer is a pound of his own flesh. If the loan is not paid back, the creditor (Shylock) gets to hurt the debtor (Antonio). While we might now think of Shylock's request as unusually barbaric, Nietzsche's historical claim is that these kinds of arrangements were once very common.

Supposing such agreements were indeed very common – one of many controversial historical claims in *GM* – then two points follow. First, what does their frequency tell us about how those who made the deals were thinking? We might expect the guarantee on a loan to be something of the same financial value. Suppose a home-owner borrows money for a car, promising to pay the money back in a year. The creditor asks what the guarantee is, what will happen if 'the ships don't come in' and the creditor can't pay it pack. The homeowner might offer the creditor, as a guarantee, a stake in the home worth more than the car. But why would a creditor accept hurting the debtor as such a guarantee? One obvious reason is that it is a deterrent: the debtor won't want to get hurt. But another reason, Nietzsche suggests, is that *hurting the debtor will be fun* (*GM* II 5–6). Taking a pound of flesh from Antonio is worth three thousand ducats because it will be such a good time for Shylock. Nietzsche is talking about the distant past, so he can accept that *you, now,* might not be interested in that kind of deal. But part of Nietzsche's point is that the historical record (allegedly) preserves evidence of the widespread understanding that there is pleasure in cruelty. It is just obvious from the prevalence of these deals that plenty of people did in fact take pleasure in hurting others. The modern reader's likely queasiness at the prospect can be absorbed into Nietzsche's argument: the historical development of Christian morality is contingent on pleasures that are *immoral* by the standards of that morality. *You* (modern, Christian reader) might not accept hurting the debtor as a guarantee on your loan. But one *cause* of your refusal is that so many other debtors before you *were* willing to accept such terms. As it happens, then, we (Christians) got the morality we have in part because our predecessors were so Christian-immoral. Incidentally, Nietzsche also holds that modern Christians are cruel, just in a more subtle way (*GM* II 6; also, *BGE* 229).

The third element of the second essay is a claim about the psychology of early humans compared with modern humans. Once upon a time, he supposes, early, transient human populations needed to be aggressive to stay alive: they needed to catch their own prey, fight off competitors and defend themselves against predators. Then, something about their living condition changed dramatically: they settled down in larger groups. Once larger groups of humans settle together, there is less of a need for the kind of aggression just described: many people in such communities do not catch their own prey and are not directly threatened by predators and competitors. In Nietzsche's own striking analogy, settled human beings are like the first fish who climb out of water to begin dwelling on land: many ages of development have honed their instincts to be perfectly appropriate for water, and now those same instincts are not only useless, but harmful, when they find themselves dealing with earth and air (*GM* II 16). Similarly, then, settled and more peaceful human populations don't need as much of their aggression, but the instincts remain. Where, as it were, does this excess aggression *go*? It cannot be taken out on predators because there aren't enough around, nor on other members of the community, on whom one now depends to stay alive. Nietzsche's answer: it turns *inward* (*GM* II 16). This self-directed aggression and cruelty is 'bad conscience in its beginnings' (*GM* II 17). Nietzsche goes on to describe this settling and inward-focused aggression as a consequence of domination, by masters, of a subordinate population in the formation of a 'state': it is only the subordinated who experience this early form of bad conscience, because only they are prevented from expressing their aggression in the usual way (*GM* II 17). Although Nietzsche speaks of 'bad conscience', it is important to see that it doesn't, initially, have anything to do with conscience as purported knowledge that one has done something wrong. It is merely an animal drive to hack away at something, directed at oneself, for want of any better, external object.

Nietzsche weaves these three elements together. If pain makes us remember, then people who are hurt when they default on their loans are likely to remember that association. In general, a cultural memory arises: defaulting on a debt leads to pain. But those suffering from the early form of bad conscience are, in fact, *seeking out* ways to be aggressive towards themselves. Ultimately, it is in the interest of such people to place themselves in relations of debt that cannot be paid off because debt leads to pain, and in this case a self-inflicted pain, 'self-torture' (*GM* II 21). In the end, the relations of debt become religious and morally charged. We owe God and we cannot pay him back: 'debt towards *God*: this thought becomes an instrument of torture' (*GM* II 22). Nietzsche therefore casts religious obligation, especially Christian obligation, as a kind of debt to God which cannot be paid off. But *what* do we owe God? The destruction of our animal nature, denial of the will (*GM* II 22, 24) – in other words, being anti-Life. It won't be possible to destroy, completely, our animal nature, but the point is to *try* because the act of trying amounts to an infinite, inner outlet for aggression. While we might not currently think of Christianity as presenting a creditor/

debtor relationship between God and human beings, it is worth noting that what Christians call the 'New *Testament*' ought really to be the 'New *Covenant*' or 'new deal', in contrast with (what Christians take to be) the 'Old Testament', that is, the previous arrangement or agreement. God makes a deal with his people, through Moses; through Jesus, he substantially revises the terms. In both cases, Nietzsche could argue, we are the debtors, while God is the creditor.

Like the first essay, the second essay portrays Life in action. Insofar as 'Life functions essentially in an injurious, violent, exploitative and destructive manner' (*GM* II 11), this is on display in the debt/pain story, where humans take pleasure in hurting others. It is also present in the bad conscience story, in which people are fundamentally and unavoidably aggressive, to others or themselves. Nietzsche suggests that the attitudes that are forced inwards – 'animosity, cruelty, the pleasure of pursuing, raiding, changing and destroying' (*GM* II 16) – can more or less be equated with 'will to power' (*GM* II 18).

The second essay also shows obfuscation in action. Christian-moral historians and scientists have been reluctant to look at Life's workings squarely in the face, precisely because that would mean acknowledging that their moral, egalitarian or democratic outlooks run counter to how things necessarily are (*GM* II 11–12; also, *GM* I 4). This may be one reason why moderns have been reluctant to acknowledge the cruelty that underpins the notion of conscience. This pleasure-bringing cruelty is nonetheless on display through history, openly in ancient festivals and more covertly in Nietzsche's own day (*GM* II 6; also, *BGE* 229). Christian morality makes us shy away from recognising cruelty's all-pervasiveness. This shying away makes it easier, in turn, to deny cruelty as a feature of Life and to interpret conscience in a more benign manner. Nietzsche tells a similar story about theories of justice: operating with Christian-moral assumptions, rival historians fail to recognise the workings of 'lust for mastery, greed and the like' that 'are of much greater biological value' (*GM* II 11).

5.3 *GM* III: The Triumph of Asceticism

It is in the third essay that Nietzsche draws everything together to explain how we ended up with a morality that is (at least apparently) anti-Life. The essay's slogan, repeated with slight variation at the start and the end, is that 'man [. . .] prefers to *will nothingness* than *not* will' (*GM* III 28; similarly, *GM* III 1). The third essay broadly follows the Impossible Strategy: Christian ascetic morality, while apparently anti-Life, is shown to be a strategy on Life's behalf. The ascetic *does* will something very strongly, as all living things must, but, unlike most living things, he wills the eradication of his own will. Now, as it happens, will-eradication is *not possible*, exactly because the attempt to do so is always the result of will, and therefore Life. Rather than being real ascetics ('not willing'), apparent ascetics are those who most certainly do will. It's just that, as it happens, what they will is 'nothingness', the destruction of will, and therefore of Life. In effect, the third essay looks at a series of contenders for those who really impede Life, and in each case Life is shown to be pulling the strings behind the scenes: apparent ascetics are people who prevent themselves from getting what they want, just to get other things that Life wants. As we have seen, he notes that some philosophers look as though they are ascetics because they shy away from marriage ('Heraclitus, Plato, Descartes, Spinoza, Leibniz, Kant, Schopenhauer'), when in fact they are seeking out their best advantage, the best conditions to pursue their work (*GM* III 7). Christians who apparently act out of neighbourly love are *really* governed by will to power, 'the strongest, most life-affirming impulse', because helping others ensures a stamp of superiority over them (*GM* III 18). But the most important ascetic in this story is the Christian priest.

We left the slaves, in the first essay, in what looked like a good way: they had told themselves that they were good and that their masters were evil. But things aren't so rosy after all. For one thing, we can now imagine that the slaves, as a settled, oppressed group, suffer from self-directed aggression. It would be good if they could find a way to resolve this. But one more Nietzschean assumption must be placed in the background before the final act: the search for meaningful suffering. Nietzsche holds that pain and suffering are not, in themselves, the most difficult things for human beings. More difficult, he supposes, is suffering that lacks any *meaning* (*GM* II 7; *GM* III 28). Imagine that Joan is an athlete in training for a race. Joan will experience plenty of acute, physical pain. But this pain will be meaningful in three ways: first, she knows *why* she suffers (regular, intense training) and 'reasons bring relief' (*GM* III 20); second, she can answer the question 'what for?' (*GM* III 20) – she suffers in relation to something she *wants* (to win); third, someone who suffers is 'yearning for cures' (*GM* III 20) and Joan has something she can *do* about her suffering (stop training). The combination of cause, purpose and means of alleviation amounts to a meaningful suffering. In Joan's case, what she believes to be the cause really is the cause, and what she thinks she could do to alleviate her suffering really would alleviate her suffering. But notice that, for Nietzsche, these beliefs do not have to be *true* to give Joan's suffering meaning (*TI* Errors 5). The pain could be completely unrelated to Joan's training and, still, from her current standpoint, her suffering would be equally meaningful. Suffering without these things – unknown, purposeless and untreatable – is the hardest to bear. Christian asceticism, we shall see, turns out to be the best meaning-giving system going (*GM* III 23, 28).

Let us look at where things stand with the slaves. They are suffering, of course: they are unhealthy and powerless. True, they can tell themselves that they are good, but the overall situation is unsatisfactory in three respects:

1. Their own suffering does not have meaning. Slave morality doesn't explain why being good *hurts* more than being evil. Shouldn't being good feel better than this?
2. The slaves (i) are primed to look for bad deals – an opportunity to express their aggressive drives on themselves and (ii) experience the psychological discomfort of seeking to be cruel to themselves.
3. The priests, meanwhile, are portrayed as looking for power over the slaves.

All this is resolved in one deft but highly consequential change. Rather than seeing the masters as evil and the slaves as good, the priests encourage the slaves to see everyone, including themselves, as evil, as sinful, and to identify being sinful with being natural. Earlier, we saw that the slaves of the first essay were motivated by '*ressentiment*' (resentment) of their masters. In *GM* III, the priest appears as the '*direction-changer of ressentiment*' (*GM* III 15), switching its focus from the master to the slave. Under the priestly revision, the urge for self-directed cruelty is reinterpreted as evidence of *sin*. The new deal, provided by the priest, is that natural instincts are sinful (*GM* II 22), that Life is sinful, and ought to be opposed. In other words, to be good is to be *anti-Life* – but, at the same time, and not accidentally, *nobody* can really be anti-Life. The slave is set up to fail.

We can think of the resulting situation as a perpetual motion machine, which resolves the three problematic elements identified previously. The slave suffers physiologically and psychologically; he looks for a meaning from the priest, who thereby gains power (3) and who provides an explanation and a cure (1); the explanation is the slave's guilty nature, the evidence for this guilty nature lying in his conscience (in fact an appeal to, and misinterpretation, of 2 (ii)); the remedy is to punish himself, crush his own nature, so he gets to take out his aggression on himself (2(i)); he suffers more, looks for explanation, and goes back to the start. *All* suffering is now captured within an elaborate system of meaning: you suffer because you sin (i.e., are Life-driven); you can always do something about it (self-mortification, attempts at Life-denial); the suffering is folded into a project, to become will-free, anti-natural, as sinless as possible. Nietzsche is quick to note that much of the story the slave adopts is, as a matter of fact, not in touch with reality. But his point is that we are meaning-seekers, not necessarily truth-seekers, and, in Christian asceticism, the slaves find a first-rate system of meaning. Hence, the claims of all three essays are drawn together, as the slaves take on an (at least apparently) anti-Life morality. This morality morphs into various subsequent, non-Christian forms of Christian morality, including the scholarly outlook, Kantian and Schopenhauerian philosophy, political egalitarianism and so on (see Section 2).

GM III portrays Life in action. The conclusion rests upon the idea that the Will (Life) always operates: apparent not-willing reveals a will that has been forced to choose nothingness. Philosophers, priests, meaning-seekers – all are Life-governed. The sickly and weak, as they take control over the healthy and strong, are driven by will to power and are very successful: 'where can it not be found, this will to power of precisely the weakest! In particular, the sick woman: nobody can outdo her refinements in ruling, oppressing, tyrannizing' (*GM* III 14). Even as the priest is encouraging anti-natural morality by blaming the 'sinners' for their suffering, Nietzsche describes this quite explicitly as something that 'the healing instinct of Life has at least *tried* to do through the ascetic priest' (*GM* III 16). This, indeed, is the point of the investigation – to figure out why Life turns (apparently) anti-Life in the ascetic priest: 'It must be a necessity of the first rank which makes this species grow and prosper when it is *hostile to Life, – Life itself must have an interest*' (*GM* III 11; also *GM* III 13). As we have seen, describing how Life has a stake in (at least apparently) anti-Life activity is an important function of *GM*, and of Nietzsche's late philosophy in general. The third essay also shows obfuscation in action. First, while suffering of all kinds is given a meaning, this meaning requires a systematic *misunderstanding* of what suffering really is, so that supernatural, rather than natural causes are sought (*GM* III 20). Second, as we saw, philosophers and priests will be inclined to be hostile to the senses and to deny the significance of the real world (*GM* III 10–12).

Nietzsche's history, as expected, is guided by the goals we set out in Section 4. Now that we have some of the details in mind, we can examine whether he achieves them.

6 Does the History Achieve Its Goals?

Earlier, I set out three aims of Nietzsche's history: to persuade the reader that Life works as Nietzsche claims; to show how we ended up with the morality that we have; to persuade us to adopt a Life-affirming morality. This part critically examines his analysis in light of these goals, looking at each goal in turn.

6.1 Demonstrating the Life Theory

As we have seen, Nietzsche's histories offer a sustained attempt to persuade the reader that Life works as Nietzsche claims. As well they should: Nietzsche's late ethical project stands or falls with the Life Theory. Life is in action in the formation of both master and slave moralities, in the formation of bad conscience, in our predilection for bad deals and, of course, in our preference for willing the destruction of our own will. Life works through the priest to try to sequester the weak, through the philosopher to keep him unmarried and through the creditor-debtor relations that ground Judeo-Christian theology. Nietzsche's repeated presentation of obfuscation in action adds to his case: we see not only that Life operates, but also why we have been inclined and incentivised not to acknowledge that fact.

Is the Life Theory thereby demonstrated, or at least convincingly supported by the history? A number of different questions arise: Are Nietzsche's historical, psychological and biological claims sufficiently determinate to be demonstrably true or false? If so, are they true? Most importantly, if true, do they reveal the workings of Life, or are there better explanations? After all, one might agree that a revolution in morals occurred with the advent of Jewish monotheism, or that humans seem to direct aggression towards themselves, while disagreeing that this has anything to with Life. I do not offer a thorough investigation here. A modern reader is unlikely to be persuaded and the question of whether Nietzsche's contemporaries would have been persuaded is more historical than philosophical. I focus more closely on the two remaining aims because these offer greater opportunities for philosophical exploration.

6.2 How Did We End Up with an Anti-Life Morality? (Or, Why Do the Masters Convert?)

We might think of Nietzsche's history as comprising four stages: the invention of Christianity and Christian morality; the spread of Christian morality, beyond its Jewish origins, to non-Jewish 'slaves'; the conversion of Roman and barbarian masters; Christian morality after the end of the Christian faith. Of these stages, we have looked at the first in detail. Nietzsche also has a story about the second: Christianity unifies the weak and oppressed under its banner. Paul presents Jesus – falsely, by all means – as a god who represents, and dies for, all the downtrodden, uniting slavelike peoples of all kinds against the Roman order (*A* 58). Jumping ahead to the fourth: Christian asceticism outlives Christianity (which it helps to destroy) and transforms into various modern ideas such as democracy, liberalism, pessimistic philosophy and the scholarly outlook. But what about the third stage, when the masters, or at least many of them, get converted? Why do the eagles become lambs? It has been suggested that a good account of why the masters convert is missing in the texts (Hatab 2011). This seems to be a major gap in the story because we are left wondering how Christian morality moved from appealing to some *against* others, to appealing to almost everyone in Europe, despite occasional flowerings of the master morality with the Renaissance and, later, Napoleon (*GM* I 16; *EH* CW 2).

We do not find a clear, dedicated analysis of the masters' conversion. However, this does not make it futile to take a closer look. There is more to say about, first, why Nietzsche might be relatively quiet and, second, the most prominent explanations in the texts. First, on the question of Nietzsche's relative silence, we can see that, like the question of whether slave morality is natural or anti-natural, this is a particularly difficult question for Nietzsche to answer. For this is another moment when he is called to square the circle. If, as per the Impossible Strategy, the masters are simply overpowered by the priests, then the priests are *better,* more Life-promoting, than the masters. If, as per the Unethical Strategy, the priests really are anti-Life, then a clear description of how they overcome the masters would presumably involve a description of Life *not fully* in action, of Life going astray or failing to achieve its goals as best it can. We have already seen the priests described in both ways (Section 3).

What explanations does Nietzsche offer for the conversion of the masters? One *prima facie* reason might be that Christian morality gives meaning for suffering, even in the masters. In *GM* III 28, the idea seems to be that Christian asceticism is the first historical instance of a meaning for suffering, that man had 'no meaning up to now'. If even the masters were lacking meaning prior to Christian asceticism, then Christianity had something important to offer them. A closer look at the texts suggests this is not Nietzsche's story, or at least not in its entirety. In various places, Nietzsche also seems to say that pre-Christian ancients *did* have meaning for their suffering (*GM* II 7), that meaning-making is something we do automatically anyway (*TI* Errors 5), that pre-Christian barbarians did not even *register or acknowledge* their suffering until it got reinterpreted in Christian terms, so they did not require meaning (*A* 22–3) and, finally, that Buddhism provides an instructive instance of a readiness to endure suffering *without* meaning (*A* 23).

Other suggestions are more closely attested in the texts. We find hints of gruesome conversion techniques and an emphasis on weakening, sickening and poisoning (*GM* P 6; *GM* I 9; *GM* III 14–15; *A* 22; *TI* Improvers 2). Without more detail, though, the idea of weakening or sickening does not help us very much. How does this happen and why does it work? The first, and most prominent, answer would generally be captured by the notion of *proximity*: the masters are insufficiently separate or apart from the slaves and priests. We might recall that masters identify themselves as good through features that mark them out in contrast to slaves. Nietzsche often emphasises the importance of the 'ruling caste' (*BGE* 257) having something or someone to look down on. His general term for this is the 'pathos of distance' (*BGE* 257; *GM* I 2; *GM* III 14). In *GM*, this felt distance between master and slave enables the masters to produce the concept of good (vs. bad) (*GM* I 2). On the one hand, then, masters need to *see* their opposites to have the appropriate self-regard. On the other hand, it seems, masters are better off separated and solitary (*GM* III 18). Indeed, *GM* I 11, somewhat confusingly given the 'pathos of distance' requirement, prefers to present the masters as producing a concept of good completely independently of the slaves. Whether the masters require complete absence or appropriate distance, what they have in fact had is close and constant proximity to the slaves' suffering, which leads to feelings of guilt and pity on their part, feelings that make them doubt themselves. Nietzsche often emphasises the psychological responses arising from close proximity to weakness and sickness: disgust, pity and guilt, for example. He thinks the *sight* of such people can function as an 'objection' to Life (*TI* Skirmishes 36; also *A* 7): '['these weak and incurably sick people'] promenade in our midst like living reproaches, like warnings to us – as though health, success, strength, pride and the feeling of power were in themselves depravities' (*GM* III 14). These are feelings that are aroused by being in the presence, and under the evocative gaze, of the 'born misfit' (Missgebornen von Anbeginn) and Nietzsche also presents the production of such affects as a strategy on the part of the weak (*GM* III 14). Consequently, one of the things that Life is initially trying to do, through the priests, is to keep the sick packed together and apart from the healthy – an aim of which Nietzsche clearly approves (*GM* III 16). However, a damaging consequence of Christian ideas, he thinks, is that they have resulted in there being more sick people around, who are permitted to reproduce and, on Christian-moral grounds, are forbidden from committing suicide (*TI* Skirmishes 36). Thoughts of this kind, in part, motivate his idea that, put simply, doctors ought to at least indirectly encourage certain patients to end their own lives so that those patients no longer present, to those around them, an objection to Life (*TI* Skirmishes 36; also, *EH* BT 4). Likely, he takes these two factors to be mutually reinforcing: being around the weak and sick encourages guilt at being healthy and furthers Christian morality; conversely, as Christian morality gains a stronger hold, getting rid of the weak and the sick becomes increasingly difficult because it is seen as immoral.

The idea of proximity still omits to tell us how or why masters are susceptible to these affects. If master morality has it that slaves are just unlucky, why should seeing these unlucky ones up close make any difference? One thought might be that these affects are natural or universal, but Nietzsche seems to want to say the opposite: pity is anti-natural and anti-Life (*A* 7). Again: Where does the susceptibility come from?

A second explanation clearly connects with the first, and it does offer a causal explanation of sorts. Nietzsche appeals to a common trope of nineteenth-century philosophy: race-mixing (Bernasconi 2010, especially pp. 503–9). Any discussion of Nietzsche and race is complicated by a number of factors: the history and legacy of European racism; the National Socialists' use and veneration of Nietzsche and, as a consequence, the postwar attempts at a rehabilitation of Nietzsche's image; the ambiguities of the term 'race' (and related terms like 'breeding') both in Nietzsche's texts and in his intellectual context; Nietzsche's inconsistencies and the changes in his thought; and the subsequent fixing of the term 'race' in a particular way, sometime after Nietzsche stopped writing (Schank 2000; Bernasconi 2010, 2017; Geuss 2019; and see the relevant parts of Sommer 2019, e.g. pp. 105–19, 2016, 575–8). To take one example: the pervasive influence of Lamarckianism, the doctrine that environmental factors directly cause changes in individuals, which are subsequently *passed on directly* to their offspring, meant that a sharp distinction between nature and culture, as occurred in later 'race' theory, was not as prominent (Bernasconi 2010, 510). For all these reasons, this discussion proceeds cautiously and does not attempt to get to the bottom of Nietzsche's particular kind or kinds of 'race' theory, nor how, if at all, he distinguishes between 'races'. I shall keep 'race' in scare quotes to prevent an easy slide to thinking of the term anachronistically.

For our purposes, the point is this: exegetically, it is a highly plausible reading of Nietzsche that he thinks interbreeding of master and slave 'races' in Europe contributed to the spread of slave morality. He has two slightly different thoughts here. The first begins with the idea that different 'races' lie behind different European classes. The dominant class can be traced back to an invading 'race' who 'hurled themselves upon weaker, more civilized, more peaceful races' (*BGE* 257; also, *BGE* 208; *GM* II 17). It follows, of course, that, *within* what would subsequently be called 'white', nineteenth-century European society, Nietzsche is suggesting that there exist different 'races' or the descendants of different 'races'. He follows various contemporary 'race' theorists (Sommer 2019, 111–14) in supposing that, in Europe, a blond and fair Aryan 'master-race' originally came to dominate a darker population (*GM* I 5; *KSA* 13: 14[195]), although he clearly allows for non-'Aryan' masters in non-European contexts (*GM* I 11). Simply put, one suggestion in the late works is that, because 'race'-mixing entails the mixing and passing on of 'qualities and preferences' (*BGE* 264), 'mixing the races up' (*GM* I 9) has weakened or poisoned the masters, passing on slave ideals to their offspring. ('Mixing the races up', in *GM* I 9, is not uttered in Nietzsche's own voice, but rather by a speaker who summarises Nietzsche's views, but with whom Nietzsche expresses some disagreement. This remark is, as I read it, part of the summary that Nietzsche endorses.) Nietzsche's hypothesis is that, in Europe, the 'subject race has ended up by regaining the upper hand in skin colour, shortness of forehead and perhaps even in intellectual and social instincts' (*GM* I 5) and he asks whether 'the conquering *master race*, that of the Aryans, is not physiologically being defeated as well?' (GM I 5; again, see Sommer 2019, 114 for Nietzsche's sources). In the context of the opposition between master and slave, Nietzsche writes that 'biologically, modern man represents a contradiction of values [. . .]. [A]ll of us have, unconsciously, in our bodies, words, formulas, moralities of *opposite* descent – we are, physiologically considered, *false*' (*CW*, Epilogue; also, *BGE* 260). As 'racially' mixed people, we are, consequently, morally mixed people.

Second, Nietzsche frequently characterises contemporary Europe as the product of *sudden, uncontrolled* 'race'-mixing, something he associates with its 'democratic' ideals, presumably because democracy treats all individuals the same way, regardless of 'race' (*BGE* 224; see also *BGE* 208, *BGE* 244). Nietzsche has various ideas about the consequences of this uncontrolled 'race'-mixing, some positive, most negative (*GS* 377; *BGE* 200, 208, 224, 251; *GM* III 17). But in *GM* III 17, sudden 'race'-mixing is one cause of the suffering that Christian morality is brought in to address. Through 'race'-mixing, then, the masters get more slavelike and they come to suffer in ways that Christian morality purports to alleviate.

Proximity and 'race'-mixing are related in Nietzsche's mind, and not just because groups who are kept apart cannot interbreed. In *GM* I 11, when he mentions the conversion of the masters ('the noble races and their ideals were finally wrecked and overpowered'), a link is forged between proximity (the negative impact of 'the disgusting spectacle of the failed, the stunted, the wasted away and the poisoned') and 'race'-mixing and the consequent resurgence of the 'pre-Aryan population' in Europe. The suggestion appears to be that the pre-Aryans, who are on the rise, are also the failed and stunted who represent 'decline'. Later, Nietzsche praises what he calls the 'Manu Law-Book' (*A* 57) – that is, supposedly, the Hindu text, *Manusmriti*, though in fact it is nothing of the sort (see Sommer 2013, 265–70, 2012, 365–71) – and contrasts it favourably with modern Europe. It is telling that, in doing so, Nietzsche claims that different natural 'castes', corresponding to different natural, physiological types, are kept carefully apart from one another by Manu, with a result that is supposedly beneficial to all concerned. It is only natural that, for someone with this kind of outlook, interest would be maintained in the idea of organised control of who is permitted to reproduce, and with whom, with a view to 'the breeding [Züchtung] of a new caste that will rule Europe' (BGE 251, translation altered; on Nietzsche and eugenics, see Holub 2018, 408–53).

This discussion is not intended to argue definitively that 'race'-mixing is Nietzsche's unique and fully articulated explanation of the conversion of the masters, only that, put together with other remarks on proximity, it is his most prominent hypothesis.

6.3 Confronting the Square Circle: Should We Affirm Life?

We now turn to Nietzsche's third aim, to bring about a revaluation of values, a turn, or return, to a natural, Life-affirming attitude. As we have seen, that might be a matter of, amongst other things, reorganising society; controlling the way that humans breed; encouraging some sick people to kill themselves; taking a more positive stance towards sexuality, power seeking and exploitation; or opposing egalitarianism. Whatever the specifics, the general problem was the one we set out earlier: the conflict of the strategies. Now that we have set out his claims in more detail, we can get a sense of how Nietzsche might try, at least, to confront the square circle.

As indicated, he often departs from the Impossible Strategy, suggesting, instead, that Life isn't always omnipotently acting through us for its own maximal advantage. Our value judgements, he can accordingly claim, are not governed by Life, at least at its best or healthiest or most effective. When Nietzsche tells us that Life is operating through Christians, he often adds that the kind of Life operating through them, or the kind of living thing they are, is sick or bad or weak: 'declining, debilitated, weary, condemned Life' (*TI* Morality 5; also *GM* III 13; *A* 17; *KSA* 11: 44[6], 13: 11[227]). If our value judgements are *not* completely governed by Life-at-its-best, then there is a gap between what Life might ideally choose to value through us and what we in fact, ourselves, value. So, let us suppose that Life can't always get what it wants under its own steam, as it were – it is too weak, sick, debilitated or in decline – and that Nietzsche is calling upon us to help it. What we have gained, with this step, is coherent logical space for Nietzsche's undertaking: Life has tried but not quite succeeded and Life's success is something to fight for.

As advertised in Section 3, the problem arises when we ask: So why *should* we fight for Life? Earlier, when discussing Nietzsche's meta-ethics, we considered the status of his claims about moralities (Section 2.5). He evaluated them based on how ethical they are. Now, though, we are asking about *his own* ethical claim that Life's aims ought to be furthered. Even if there is now a coherent and non-contradictory task, we must ask Nietzsche why we ought to work on Life's behalf, given that, on this line of interpretation, he admits we do not have to.

Nietzsche spends relatively little time answering this question and he offers various, unsatisfactory answers. Some passages give plausible grounds for reticence. He claims that, because all our valuations are to some degree Life-governed, the question of Life's value is simply out of bounds: the problem is 'inaccessible' (*TI* Morality 5) or (a slightly different claim) statements like 'Life is good' or 'Life is bad' (these are my own examples) 'can [...] never be true' (*TI* Socrates 2). This only makes our question more pressing: If the problem is inaccessible, why does Nietzsche place so much weight on a particular *answer* to it, namely that Life's goals ought to be furthered?

He does make some concrete suggestions. First, it is, after all, psychologically or physiologically *worse* to be Christian (*EH* D 2). If asking 'Why Life?' were equivalent to 'Why health?' or 'Why be stronger rather than weaker?' or 'Why have control?', then, plausibly, the answer would lie in the question(s). Health in particular, one might suppose, just is something that, at a most rational level, we prefer to its alternative. Of course, people knowingly make choices at the expense of their own health: Nietzsche had earlier endorsed this kind of choice and had called into question the very idea of one, universal kind of health (*GS* 120). But the later Nietzsche might respond that there is a fairly intuitive sense in which one ought not to damage one's health and that getting healthier – recovering from a cold, for example – is always, in itself, good news. A deeper problem, though, lies with Nietzsche's particular understanding of health. To most present-day readers, 'stay healthy!' would mean something like 'stay as healthy as you (individually) can!' A person with a grave and unpleasant illness would accordingly try to manage their condition as well as possible. For Nietzsche, though, as we have seen, it may well be in Life's interests, therefore it may well be healthy in the relevant sense, for such a seriously ill person to commit suicide. Health, for Nietzsche, is not (or not just) a quality of individuals: it takes into account their impact on others, on humanity as a whole. The unhealthy, as he understands them, inhibit the attractions of Life and, as we saw, proximity to them is a factor in the prevalence of Christian morality. At this point, the *self-evidence* of the attraction of staying healthy may begin to fade: killing or, at least, sequestering yourself is not as inherently appealing as getting over a cold.

A second suggestion is that the language of health implies ease, pleasure or lack of pain. If fighting on Life's behalf were a matter of having an easier or more pleasurable time of it, then we would have a fairly clear motivation for doing so. *Sometimes*, this does appear to be Nietzsche's idea (*GM* II 24; *TI* Socrates 11; *A* 11). Often, though, he says something else. At *GM* P 6, the *Christian* is 'perhaps in more comfort and less danger'. Later in that book, Nietzsche sharply distinguishes the path that Life leads 'every animal' down from the path to happiness: 'it is *not* his path to "happiness" I am talking about, but the path to power [...] and in most cases, actually, his path to misery' (*GM* III 7).

Plausibly, there is a third response in Nietzsche. He writes: '[W]hen we speak of values, we do so under the inspiration and from the perspective of

Life: Life itself evaluates through us *when* we establish values' (*TI* Morality 5; also, KSA 13: 11[96]). Nietzsche might be appealing to a kind of 'always already' argument (for reconstructions, see Richardson 2013, 772–3; Stern forthcoming; Katsafanas 2018). 'Look,' he would be telling the reader, 'you are always already on Life's side! That's just what being alive means. You just aren't helping Life as well as you could. It is as if you are trying to climb to the top of a mountain and I'm helping you get there: it hardly makes sense to try to get to the top but to refuse to do it effectively.' This reconstructed argument does not resolve things, though. For we can imagine the Christian responding as follows: 'Let us agree that, deep down, I set out to further Life's ends and that Life still operates through me; let us agree, too, that Life is dominance, violence and exploitation. But we also agree that I am indeed inhibiting Life. I choose resistance!' Nietzsche can, of course, respond that this would be a divided or alienated existence because one is knowingly driven by a motive to which one does not ultimately commit. But is anything especially wrong with being so divided? Suitably described, it sounds rather tragic-heroic, as its equivalent does, sometimes, in Schopenhauer, when he advocates resistance to Life. Moreover, our situation, as Nietzsche often portrays it, is in any case one in which some form of division is inescapable: if we are already 'biologically' split between Life and anti-Life (*CW*, Epilogue), as he suggests, then choosing one or the other, without division of some kind, is likely to be impossible.

7 Nietzsche beyond Nietzsche's Ethics

By focusing on Nietzsche's ethics, we left out some features, or purported features, of his philosophy that might look to the reader as though they clash with the views I have presented here. This last part looks at three possible candidates. Though our discussion here makes no pretence at comprehensiveness, it is fruitful to explore these ideas, not just to correct possible misunderstanding, but also because doing so affords us a brief opportunity to take a broader view of Nietzsche's philosophy in the light of his ethics.

7.1 Interpretation and Perspective

The reader familiar with some interpretations of Nietzsche might, by now, have entertained a version of the following thought: 'Doesn't Nietzsche think that all knowledge is just a perspective or a kind of subjective interpretation? And yet you have presented a philosopher who grounds his ethics on the Life Theory, a theory about the essential functioning of the organic world. Isn't that theory, and the ethics that it grounds, also just a perspective or subjective interpretation? And isn't his ethics, therefore, in some way relativized to his own perspective?'

The claim that Nietzsche has a theory usefully called 'perspectivism' is common but controversial; plenty of interpretations are available (for relevant passages, see *HH* P 6; *GS* 354, 374; *GM* III 12; for an overview of critical interpretations, see Gemes 2013; for a close, sceptical reading of *HH* P 6's supposed perspectivism, see Dellinger 2015). In the late works, he certainly makes some important remarks about the relation between Life and perspective, meaning or interpretation. In considering the relationship between Life Theory and perspective, this is the best place to start.

Although we discussed some cases of obfuscation in action in *GM* II, there is, in fact, a subtler form of it on display in that essay. As we have seen, Nietzsche claims that true understanding of biological and historical developments requires the historian to examine the power operations at work beneath the surface – the ones that Christians have a vested interest in not acknowledging (Section 5.2). The crucial, extra point for the present discussion is this: up for grabs, in this power struggle that is essential to Life, is the very meaning and purpose of that which is fought over.

In *GM* II, the example is punishment. So, adapting Nietzsche's thought, his point is that spaces like courtrooms, prisons and gallows, when controlled and described by one group of people, will be doing something very different from what those same spaces do when controlled and described by another group. Part of successful overpowering just is successful alteration of the meaning and function of whatever has been overpowered. Hence, to suppose that punishment has and has always had one and only one function is to misunderstand Life. Moreover, such a mistaken supposition would not be ethically neutral: because Christianity is currently dominant, many current interpretations and functions serve Christian morality, but that is not how they always were. Rival genealogists think of everything in terms of a single, unchanging function, which in fact happens to be the most recent, Christian one. Hence, they obscure the internecine power struggle of history operating beneath the surface, which confers only temporary meaning on the spoils of war. One of the reasons that *GM* is meant to be more successful than rival genealogies is that it takes into account this power struggle for meaning and function. Nietzsche puts this point forcefully:

> there is no more important proposition for every sort of history than that which we arrive at only with great effort [...] namely that [...] anything in existence, having somehow come about, is continually interpreted anew, requisitioned anew, transformed and redirected to a new purpose by a power superior to it; that everything that occurs in the organic world

consists of overpowering, dominating, and in turn, all overpowering and dominating is a new-interpreting, an adjustment, by which the hitherto existing 'meaning' and 'purpose' must necessarily be obscured or completely obliterated. (*GM* II 12, translation altered)

Christians have been blind to the thesis that 'a power-will is acted out in all that happens' (*GM* II 12): hence, they have failed to understand not only the specific historical functions of things, but also what a function really is – a temporary victory-flag, raised by a temporarily successful army. Whatever the relevant element – person, group, sub-personal drive, organ or cell – Nietzsche clearly thinks that successful power seeking often requires new, self-serving meanings and functions to be produced, by the victorious party, for what has been taken over, exploited and incorporated (see also *KSA* 12: 2[108]; 2[148]; 2[151]). He can therefore use the term '*interpretation*' *biologically*, so that the development of an organ involves 'interpretation' and, indeed, '*the organic process presupposes constant interpreting*' (*KSA* 12: 2[148], Nietzsche's double emphasis).

To state the obvious, far from suggesting that the Life Theory is just a perspective, these passages about the power struggle for meaning and interpretation *presuppose and do not call into question* the Life Theory. Nietzsche moves from an understanding of the Life-driven 'organic process' to a theory of 'constant interpreting'. We, readers of Nietzsche, would be within our rights to ask him: Where does the Life Theory belong in this power struggle for meaning, interpretation and function? Is the Life Theory or, we might say more pointedly, Nietzsche's *interpretation* of the organic realm as power struggle supposed to have a special status, so that the true nature and the correct interpretation of Life is no longer up for grabs in the general struggle for power and meaning? Or is Nietzsche's interpretation of Life, itself, transitory, provisional, merely an expression of Nietzsche's own 'power-will'? Neither answer – that it has a protected status or that it does not – seems satisfactory without further elaboration. If the Life Theory is protected, then how and why is Nietzsche's philosophising somehow exempt from Life's grip on interpretation? If his Life Theory does not have protected status, then what now grounds the idea that there is such a thing as the struggle for meaning, interpretation and function in the first place? We have thrown the baby out with the bathwater.

In line with the method of this study, and especially because perspective is not our focus, we need not explore or propose a philosophical solution to this dilemma. But, exegetically, there is an answer: Nietzsche never, to my knowledge, *explicitly* turns the thought around on himself. That is, he never argues that the conclusion undermines or calls into question the meaning or validity of the Life Theory. Instead, he always starts with the Life Theory and, from there, moves to the competition for meaning, with the Life Theory left untouched. In one note, for example, he writes that 'previous interpretations have been perspectival appraisals by means of which we preserve ourselves in life, that is, in the will to power and to the growth of power' (*KSA* 12: 2[108]). Theory of interpretation follows on from, and does not rebound upon, Life Theory. In a note which is often taken to state 'perspectivism', he concludes that our 'drives' do the interpreting, where 'every drive is a kind of lust for domination' (*KSA* 12: 7[60]). Again, Life (lust for domination) requires interpretative activity, but the Life Theory is not presented as open to interpretation. In the most famous (and notoriously difficult) statement of his so-called perspectivism, the Life Theory also looks to be present in the background: he writes that any supposed account of the subject as a knower in whom 'the active and interpretative powers are to be suppressed' – he is thinking of Schopenhauer's view, amongst others – is an 'absurdity' and he concludes that 'there is *only* a perspectival seeing, *only* a perspectival knowing' (*GM* III 12). Recall that the 'active and interpretative powers' belong to Life. Recall, too, that Nietzsche is on the lookout for any Christian-moral outlook that rejects an X that is an essential condition of Life. Our active and interpretative powers are just such an X: in asking us to be without them, the Schopenhauerian is, as expected, making a Christian, anti-Life move. Nietzsche is not calling into question his Life Theory, saying that it is merely a perspective. He is invoking his account of Life, *using* it to justify a criticism of other theories as anti-Life.

The point of this discussion is not to resolve any questions about perspectivism, interpretatively or philosophically. The reader is merely cautioned against thinking that, for example, because Nietzsche purportedly thinks that there is only a perspectival knowing (or some similar formulation), Nietzsche clearly means to suggest that his own Life Theory and the ethics that it grounds are 'only perspectival' in a way that is intended to call their validity into question. There is no evidence for that in his texts.

7.2 Truth and Error

Another association the reader may bring to Nietzsche is that he thought of error or falsehood as somehow all-pervasive and essential. Indeed, this, or something like it, is exactly what he thought, including in the late works. If Nietzsche did think that error is deep-seated, necessary, baked-in, as it were, to cognition, then surely this undermines his purportedly true account of Life? Is the Life Theory not also somehow erroneous?

Given our focus on his ethics, there is an easy answer to this and a difficult answer. The easy answer is that *any* exegesis of Nietzsche on any topic, including on truth, is likely to struggle to incorporate his sceptical remarks about truth. If, as Nietzsche seems to suggest, *any* use of 'unity, identity, duration, substance, cause, materiality [and] being' (*TI* Reason 5) necessitates error, then good luck producing an interpretation of Nietzsche's ethical theory, or of his theory of anything else, which is not, by his standards, error ridden. The difficulty of squaring will to power with the denial of substance provides a good example (Bittner 2000). There is a great deal more to say about *why* Nietzsche makes these claims, including philosophical influences and arguments that have gone unexplored here (Green 2002; Hussain 2004; Anderson 2005; Scheibenberger 2016). My point is only that Nietzsche's views about error ought not to be wheeled out casually against a particular interpretation, when they would cause problems for any interpretation.

There is also a more difficult and speculative answer, which can only be sketched here. It begins with two reasonably secure exegetical points, but the speculative move is to unite them. First, Nietzsche partly draws his error theory *from* his account of Life: Life needs or requires error. Why and how? Nietzsche is likely building on suggestions from earlier texts (*BT, OTL, UM II, GS* 110–12), but one idea was that certain errors provide an evolutionary advantage (*GS* 110). Second, Nietzsche bases his error theory, in part, on a theory of absolute becoming: reality, he sometimes suggests, is, at its deepest level, a kind of constant flux or change (*KSA* 9: 11[162]; *KSA* 12: 9[98]; *GS* 107). But, so the argument went (sound or otherwise), cognition is a matter of fixed statements using fixed concepts. Consequently, cognition always fails to match up to reality's constant change.

With these two elements in mind, their combination would go as follows: Nietzsche is experimenting with identifying reality's constant becoming with Life's constant power struggle and contest, hence: '*a quantum of power*, a becoming' (*KSA* 13: 11[73]). (It may help to recall Nietzsche's entertaining of the idea that will to power governs not merely the organic realm, but also, in some sense, the ultimate reality [*BGE* 36].) The philosopher's hostility to the senses is elsewhere recast as a form of hostility to becoming (*TI* Reason 1–2). Philosophy (before Nietzsche) has imposed fixity on becoming and has thereby erred. Nietzsche, here, uses imagery and terminology associated with the Life Theory: 'nothing actual has escaped from their hands alive'; they treat 'procreation and growth' (among other typical features of Life) as 'objections' (*TI* Reason 1). One can therefore see Nietzsche as identifying hostility to the reality of becoming with hostility to the reality of Life. The suggestion is not that this speculative combination solves any problem of how Nietzsche can reconcile his views about error with his views about ethics. It is that the text hints that his ethics and his views about error may be thought of as two branches growing from the same trunk: Life and absolute becoming are the same thing; philosophy's hostility to absolute becoming equates to hostility to Life. Perhaps the force of the error theory is not meant to be applied to the Life Theory.

7.3 Art, Self-Creation and Value Creation

Nietzsche has often been described as a theorist of self-cultivation or self-creation and, generally, as one who encourages us to take an aesthetic or artistic attitude towards self and world (most famously in Nehamas 1985). The reader might therefore wonder how a philosopher who espouses radical, aesthetic self-creation, including the creation of values, could offer a universal, nature-based ethics.

In fact, one could imagine self-creation of a limited kind occurring in the context of Nietzsche's late ethics. Importantly, though, such self-creation could not extend to the creation of fundamental *values*, which are, after all, fixed by Life. Hence, in the autobiographical *EH*, Nietzsche by all means presents himself as a shaper of his own life, but not as an *inventor* of values: they are there to be found in nature, and Nietzsche's significance lies in his ability to reveal them in the face of Christian hostility and obfuscation (*EH* Destiny). The same is true for other late passages that are sometimes exhibited as instances of ethical self-creation: when Nietzsche praises Goethe, for example, it is explicitly in the context of Nietzsche's ideas about nature and Life (*TI* Skirmishes 48–9). Why might some have claimed that Nietzsche asks us to create our own values? This is a case in which a lack of attention to the changes in Nietzsche's thought has produced confusing results. There is no denying that Nietzsche does advocate forms of artistic value creation, and self-cultivation of a more fundamental kind, but it is hard to find passages to that effect in the late works, especially after *BGE*, which might best be read as transitional in that regard. The most famous passages are usually from *UM* or *GS* I–IV (*GS* 107, 276, 290, 299, 301).

As regards art and beauty in particular, the later Nietzsche makes various attempts to ground them in the Life Theory. *GM* II 18 has our interest in beauty as arising from bad conscience: self-directed aggression, a form of will to power, makes us find ourselves ugly, and therefore form the opposite conception of the beautiful. In *TI* Skirmishes 19–20, beauty is the affirmation of health, while ugliness is disgust at degeneration. As for art, Nietzsche praises it, in this period, primarily because he takes it to be a celebration of lying and deception – things that (we have seen) are essential to Life and, relatedly, are opposed by Christian morality (*GM* III 25). Setting aside the question of how these claims might fit together into a cogent aesthetic theory, the point, for our purposes, is that they are alike in attempting to slot art and beauty into the framework of the Life Theory. The late Nietzsche is not a theorist of the artist or creative self as a source of independent values, but only insofar as they are bounded by his universal, biological ethics.

Conclusion: The Future of Nietzschean Ethics?

The Nietzschean ethics presented here are tied to a specific time, place and intellectual context: arguments about pessimism, nineteenth-century biological science, theories of 'race' and Schopenhauerian philosophy. It is not, perhaps, a very useful or sensitive metric, when assessing historical figures who operated with very different assumptions, to ask whether their theory is flatly right or wrong by present-day standards. Nonetheless, I trust I have indicated what the answer would be to such a question, should anyone be forced to give one.

It might be more helpful to break down Nietzsche's ethical theory into different dimensions. In general, this study has not dwelt on exactly how to categorise Nietzsche's ethics, preferring to use its pages to explain what his views are than to ask which of various inadequate or ill-defined categories best applies. But if we wish to conclude by reflecting on the prospects of his kind of view, a word on categorisation seems appropriate: After all, what is his *kind* of view?

Nietzsche's ethics, as we have set them out, combine a number of elements that might be taken apart and considered in isolation.

A. Aristotelian Moral Naturalism

The Life Theory presents a supposed natural fact about the kind of beings we are: power-seekers. The Normative Command tells us to be natural, to be the kind of beings that we naturally are, in the best possible way. Though it would hardly capture the twists and turns of Nietzsche's own meta-ethical remarks (Section 6.3), one intuitive way to step back and categorise such a view would be as a form of Aristotelian moral naturalism. According to such a view, a good thing is one that successfully performs its function. Nietzsche evidently holds that there are natural facts about good human functioning and that to be ethical is to perform that natural function well. It goes without saying that Nietzsche's Aristotelianism is not the same as Aristotle's.

B. Ethics and Evolution

Nietzsche's Life Theory, as I have presented it, is an evolutionary theory, so long as one remembers that 'evolutionary' and 'Darwinian' are not synonyms. The ethics he builds on the Life Theory are evolutionary ethics: the Life Theory accounts for how we got our morality and it also tells us how we ought to behave, that is, in accordance with how we have evolved to behave. Nietzsche's arguments, here, are in explicit dialogue with other evolutionary ethicists such as Spencer and Rée.

C. Morality's historical contingency

We have already noted the Nietzschean legacy of the genealogical method – one that can be more generally applied and that need not appeal to his Life Theory (Section 4). A striking feature of his approach is that ethical theory, so he seems to imply, must take into account the contingencies that led us to adopt our particular moral views. We will be liable to parochialism and ignorant self-aggrandisement if we do not bear in mind both the reasons why others had different moral viewpoints and the accidental or even horrifying path by which we came to have our own.

D. Outspoken anti-moralism

We cannot ignore Nietzsche's status as an iconoclast who is not afraid to tell it like it is and who invites us to do the same. Nietzsche's opposition to equality and democracy, and his standpoint from which most contemporary values and outlooks are somehow misguided and dangerous, might be thought an important model, regardless of the details. Despite having an ethics, he is hostile to a contemporary morality that, he argues, does not subject itself to sufficient reflection. A colleague of mine once told me about walking back from the nursery with another parent, who was complaining about competitive parenting. The other parent asked why each child couldn't just be enjoyed equally as they are, without all the competition. 'Before I had read Nietzsche,' my colleague said, 'I would have agreed with her. But now I thought: "you're only saying that because your son is shit!"' The appeal to equality, Nietzsche might indeed say, both flies against empirical reality and, *obviously*, is the sort of thing you are likely to be drawn to if you sense that you won't win out otherwise. The anecdote also captures a liberating quality to Nietzsche's writing. On reading Nietzsche, there are things it suddenly becomes permissible to think and say.

Each of these four dimensions is present in Nietzsche's late ethical thought and they come together to form his distinctive outlook. There are facts about our natural flourishing (A), underpinned by an evolutionary theory of sorts (B), which determine what it is to be good. Unfortunately, we moderns are (at least apparently) *not* good by this natural standard (D), and our contingent, parochial confusion can be exposed and perhaps rectified by the appropriate kind of history (C). To understand Nietzsche, we must hold all these elements together in mind. Regarding D, for example, if we are reading Nietzsche, and not merely being liberated by some of his ideas and experiments, or by an ideal bearing his name, then we must acknowledge *what* he thought it was permissible or even imperative to say, and *how* he critically, historically examined Christian morality. The *what* in question involves not just some amusingly unfashionable thoughts, but also fairly specific claims about 'race' and eugenics, some of which cannot easily be dismissed as peripheral to his ethical project; the *how* invokes his moral naturalism and evolutionary ethics.

What if we want to develop a Nietzschean ethics of our own? Then we must note that each element, in isolation, may be developed in different directions, often drawing conclusions that are very different from Nietzsche's – conclusions that may conflict with each other. Taking evolution seriously in ethical thought (B) might lead to conclusions that fit very well with Christian morality (contra D). Morality's historical contingency (C) might warn us against proclaiming that something is naturally human, when it might just be something nineteenth-century, Lutheran or bourgeois (contra A). Many neo-Aristotelians (A) endorse moral views that Nietzsche would obviously take to be 'Christian' (contra D). One could take up Nietzsche's outspoken anti-moralism (D), while disputing his version of which natural facts relate to morality (contra A) or even his understanding of what contemporary morality is (contra his specific version of C).

For Nietzsche, what prevents these four approaches from drifting apart is the Life Theory, which plays a role in all of them: it grounds the facts and the evolutionary story relating to morality; it governs the history; it provides the criterion by which modernity is held to account. The Life Theory is the anchor of Nietzsche's ethics: without it, his ethical theory is set adrift and then shattered, the pieces blown about by the prevailing winds. The spirit of Nietzsche's ethics becomes indeterminate. If we find ourselves unpersuaded by the Life Theory, then we would be better off arguing about ethics in our own right, rather than invoking Nietzsche's name.

Bibliography

Nietzsche's Works

Abbreviations and Translations

Citations of Nietzsche's works use the following abbreviations, typically followed by an aphorism number. Translations are from the listed edition, unless otherwise stated.

A = *The Antichrist [Der Antichrist]*, translated by R. J. Hollingdale. London: Penguin Classics, 1990.

BGE = *Beyond Good and Evil [Jenseits von Gut und Böse]*, translated by Walter Kaufmann in *Basic Writings of Nietzsche*. New York: The Modern Library, 2000.

BT = *The Birth of Tragedy [Die Geburt der Tragödie]*, translated by Ronald Speirs. Cambridge: Cambridge University Press, 1999.

CW = *The Case of Wagner [Der Fall Wagner]*, translated by Walter Kaufmann in *The Birth of Tragedy and The Case of Wagner*, New York: Vintage, 1967.

EH = *Ecce Homo*, translated by W. Kaufmann in *Basic Writings of Nietzsche*. New York: The Modern Library, 2000. References to this work also include an abbreviated section name.

GM = *On the Genealogy of Morality [Zur Genealogie der Moral]*, translated by Carol Diethe. Cambridge: Cambridge University Press, 1997.

GS = *The Gay Science [Die fröhliche Wissenschaft]*, translated by Josefine Nauckhoff, Cambridge: Cambridge University Press, 2001.

HH = *Human, All Too Human [Menschliches, Allzumenschliches]*, translated by R. J. Hollingdale, Cambridge: Cambridge University Press, 1996.

KSA = *Kritische Studienausgabe,* edited by Giorgio Colli and Mazzino Montinari, 15 volumes. Berlin: Walter de Gruyter, 1988. References give volume and fragment number. For example, '*KSA* 13: 11[370]' refers to the fragment entitled '11[370]' in volume 13.

OTL = 'On Truth and Lying in a Non-Moral Sense', in *The Birth of Tragedy and Other Writings*, translated by Ronald Speirs. Cambridge: Cambridge University Press, 1999.

TI = *Twilight of the Idols [Götzen-Dämmerung]*, translated by R. J. Hollingdale, London: Penguin Classics, 1990. References to this work include an abbreviated section name.

UM = *Untimely Meditations [Unzeitgemäße Betrachtungen]*, translated by R. J. Hollingdale. Cambridge: Cambridge University Press, 1997. References to this work are followed by the essay number.

Works by Other Authors

Anderson, R. Lanier. 2005. 'Nietzsche on Truth, Illusion, and Redemption'. *European Journal of Philosophy* 13 (2): 185–225.

Aschheim, Steven E. 1992. *The Nietzsche Legacy in Germany: 1890–1990.* Berkeley: University of California Press.

Beiser, Frederick C. 2016. *Weltschmerz: Pessimism in German Philosophy, 1860–1900.* New York: Oxford University Press.

Bernasconi, Robert. 2010. 'The Philosophy of Race in the Nineteenth Century'. In *The Routledge Companion to Nineteenth Century Philosophy*, edited by Dean Moyar, 498–521. London: Routledge.

2017. 'Nietzsche as a Philosopher of Racialized Breeding'. In *The Oxford Handbook of Philosophy and Race*, edited by Naomi Zack, 54–62. Oxford: Oxford University Press.

Bittner, Rüdiger. 2000. 'Masters without Substance'. In *Nietzsche's Postmoralism: Essays on Nietzsche's Prelude to Philosophy's Future*, edited by Richard Schacht, 34–46. Cambridge: Cambridge University Press.

Brobjer, Thomas H. 2008. *Nietzsche's Philosophical Context: An Intellectual Biography.* Urbana: University of Illinois Press.

2016. 'Nietzsche's Reading and Knowledge of Natural Science: An Overview'. In *Nietzsche and Science*, edited by Thomas H. Brobjer and Gregory Moore, 21–50. New York: Routledge.

Darwin, Charles. 1871. *The Descent of Man, and Selection in Relation to Sex.* Vol. 1. 2 vols. New York: Appleton.

Dellinger, Jakob. 2015. '"Du Solltest das perspektivische in jeder Werthschätzung begreifen lernen." Zum Problem des Perspektivischen in der Vorrede zu Menschliches, Allzumenschliches I'. *Nietzsche-Studien* 44 (1): 340–79.

Emden, Christian J. 2014. *Nietzsche's Naturalism: Philosophy and the Life Sciences in the Nineteenth Century.* Cambridge: Cambridge University Press.

Forster, Michael N. 2019. 'Nietzsche on Free Will'. In *The New Cambridge Companion to Nietzsche*, edited by Tom Stern, 374–96. Cambridge: Cambridge University Press.

Foucault, Michel. 1977. 'Nietzsche, Genealogy, History'. In *Language, Counter-Memory, Practice: Selected Essays and Interviews*, 139–64. Ithaca, NY: Cornell University Press.

Gemes, Ken. 2001. 'Postmodernism's Use and Abuse of Nietzsche'. *Philosophy and Phenomenological Research* 62 (2): 337–60.

2013. 'Life's Perspectives'. In *The Oxford Handbook of Nietzsche*, edited by Ken Gemes and John Richardson, 553–75. Oxford: Oxford University Press.

Geuss, Raymond. 1997. 'Nietzsche and Morality'. *European Journal of Philosophy* 5 (1): 1–20.

1999. 'Nietzsche and Genealogy'. In *Morality, Culture, and History: Essays on German Philosophy*, 1–28. Cambridge: Cambridge University Press.

2002. 'Genealogy as Critique'. *European Journal of Philosophy* 10 (2): 209–15.

2019. 'Nietzsche's Germans'. In *The New Cambridge Companion to Nietzsche*, edited by Tom Stern, 397–419. Cambridge: Cambridge University Press.

Golomb, Jacob, and Robert Wistrich, eds. 2002. *Nietzsche, Godfather of Fascism? On the Uses and Abuses of a Philosophy*. Princeton, NJ: Princeton University Press.

Green, Michael Steven. 2002. *Nietzsche and the Transcendental Tradition*. Urbana: University of Illinois Press.

Hartmann, Eduard von. 1869. *Philosophie des Unbewussten: Versuch einer Weltanschauung*. Berlin: Duncker.

Hatab, Lawrence. 2011. 'Why Would Master Morality Surrender Its Power?' In *Nietzsche's Genealogy of Morality: A Critical Guide*, edited by Simon May, 193–213. Cambridge: Cambridge University Press.

2019. 'The Will to Power'. In *The New Cambridge Companion to Nietzsche*, edited by Tom Stern, 329–50. Cambridge: Cambridge University Press.

Higgins, Kathleen, and Bernd Magnus. 1996. *The Cambridge Companion to Nietzsche*. Cambridge: Cambridge University Press.

Holub, Robert C. 2002. 'The Elisabeth Legend: The Cleansing of Nietzsche and the Sullying of His Sister'. In *Nietzsche, Godfather of Fascism?*, 215–34. Princeton, NJ: Princeton University Press.

2016. *Nietzsche's Jewish Problem: Between Anti-Semitism and Anti-Judaism*. Princeton, NJ: Princeton University Press.

2018. *Nietzsche in the Nineteenth Century: Social Questions and Philosophical Interventions*. Philadelphia: University of Pennsylvania Press.

Huenemann, Charlie. 2013. 'Nietzsche's Illness'. In *The Oxford Handbook of Nietzsche*, edited by Ken Gemes and John Richardson, 63–82. Oxford: Oxford University Press.

Hussain, Nadeem J. Z. 2004. 'Nietzsche's Positivism'. *European Journal of Philosophy* 12 (3): 326–68.

2011. 'The Role of Life in the Genealogy'. In *Nietzsche's Genealogy of Morality: A Critical Guide*, edited by Simon May, 142–69. Cambridge: Cambridge University Press.

2013. 'Nietzsche's Metaethical Stance'. In *The Oxford Handbook of Nietzsche*, edited by Ken Gemes and John Richardson, 389–412. Oxford: Oxford University Press.

Janaway, Christopher. 2007. *Beyond Selflessness: Reading Nietzsche's Genealogy*. Oxford: Oxford University Press.

Katsafanas, Paul. 2018. 'The Antichrist as a Guide to Nietzsche's Mature Ethical Theory'. In *The Nietzschean Mind*, edited by Paul Katsafanas, 83–101. London: Routledge.

Koelb, Clayton, ed. 1990. *Nietzsche as Postmodernist: Essays Pro and Contra*. Albany, NY: SUNY Press.

Kohler, Josef. 1885. *Das Recht als Kulturerscheinung. Einleitung in die vergleichende Rechtswissenschaft*. Würzburg: Stahl.

Lecky, William E. H. 1921. *History of European Morals from Augustus to Charlemagne*. Vol. 1. 2 vols. New York and London: D. Appleton.

Luchte, James, ed. 2008. *Nietzsche's Thus Spoke Zarathustra: Before Sunrise*. London and New York: Continuum.

Mainländer, Philipp. 1879. *Die Philosophie der Erlösung*. Berlin: Theodor Hofmann.

Melamed, Yitzhak Y. 2013. 'Charitable Interpretations and the Political Domestication of Spinoza, or, Benedict in the Land of the Secular Imagination'. In *Philosophy and Its History: Aims and Methods in the Study of Early Modern Philosophy*, edited by Mogens Laerke, Justin E. H. Smith, and Eric Schliesser, 258–77. Oxford: Oxford University Press.

Moore, Gregory. 2002. *Nietzsche, Biology and Metaphor*. Cambridge: Cambridge University Press.

Nehamas, Alexander. 1985. *Nietzsche: Life as Literature*. Cambridge, MA: Harvard University Press.

O'Connell, Jeffrey. 2017. 'Nietzsche's Rejection of Nineteenth-Century Evolutionary Ethics'. In *The Cambridge Handbook of Evolutionary Ethics*, edited by Robert J. Richards and Michael Ruse, 28–42. Cambridge: Cambridge University Press.

Pippin, Robert B. 1988. 'Irony and Affirmation in Nietzsche's Thus Spoke Zarathustra'. In *Nietzsche's New Seas*, edited by Tracey Strong and Michael Gillespie, 45–74. Chicago: University of Chicago Press.

2006. 'Lightning and Flash, Agent and Deed'. In *Nietzsche's* On the Genealogy of Morals: Critical Essays, edited by Christa Davis Acampora, 131–45. Lanham, MD: Rowman & Littlefield.

Porter, James I. 2013. 'Nietzsche and the Impossibility of Nihilism'. In *Nietzsche, Nihilism and the Philosophy of the Future*, edited by Jeffrey Metzger, 143–57. London: Bloomsbury Academic.

Reckermann, Alfons. 2003. *Lesarten der Philosophie Nietzsches*. Berlin and New York: De Gruyter.

Rée, Paul. 2003. 'The Origin of the Moral Sensations'. In *Basic Writings*, edited and translated by Robin Small, 85–168. Urbana: University of Illinois Press.

Richards, Robert J. 2009. 'Darwin's Theory of Natural Selection and Its Moral Purpose'. In *The Cambridge Companion to the 'Origin of Species'*, edited by Michael Ruse and Robert J. Richards, 47–66. Cambridge: Cambridge University Press.

2013. 'The German Reception of Darwin's Theory, 1860-1945'. In *The Darwin Encyclopedia*, edited by Michael Ruse, 235–42. Cambridge: Cambridge University Press.

2017. 'Evolutionary Ethics: A Theory of Moral Realism'. In *The Cambridge Handbook of Evolutionary Ethics*, edited by Robert J. Richards and Michael Ruse, 143–57. Cambridge: Cambridge University Press.

Richardson, John. 2013. 'Life's Ends'. In *The Oxford Handbook of Nietzsche*, edited by Ken Gemes and John Richardson, 127–49. Oxford: Oxford University Press.

Rolph, William Henry. 1884. *Biologische Probleme zugleich als Versuch zur Entwicklung einer rationellen Ethik*. Zweite, stark erweiterte Auflage. Leipzig: Wilhelm Engelmann.

Roux, Wilhelm. 1881. *Der Kampf der Theile im Organismus*. Leipzig: Wilhelm Engelmann.

Ruse, Michael. 2017. 'Darwinian Evolutionary Ethics'. In *The Cambridge Handbook of Evolutionary Ethics*, edited by Michael Ruse and Robert J. Richards, 89–100. Cambridge: Cambridge University Press.

Schank, Gerd. 2000. *'Rasse' und 'Züchtung' bei Nietzsche*. Berlin and Boston: De Gruyter.

Scheibenberger, Sarah. 2016. *Nietzsche-Kommentar: Ueber Wahrheit und Lüge im aussermoralischen Sinne*. Berlin and Boston: de Gruyter.

Schopenhauer, Arthur. 2014. *The World as Will and Representation, Volume 1*. Translated by Christopher Janaway, Judith Norman, and Alistair Welchman. Cambridge: Cambridge University Press.

2018. *The World as Will and Representation, Volume 2*. Translated by Christopher Janaway, Judith Norman, and Alistair Welchman. Cambridge: Cambridge University Press.

Small, Robin. 2001. *Nietzsche in Context*. Aldershot and Burlington, VT: Ashgate.

2005. *Nietzsche and Rée: A Star Friendship*. Oxford: Oxford University Press.

Sommer, Andreas Urs. 2010. 'Nietzsche mit und gegen Darwin in den Schriften von 1888'. *Nietzscheforschung: Jahrbuch der Nietzsche-Gesellschaft* 17: 31–44.

2012. *Nietzsche-Kommentar: Der Fall Wagner; Götzen-Dammerung*. Berlin and Boston: Walter de Gruyter.

2013. *Nietzsche-Kommentar: Der Antichrist; Ecce Homo; Dionysos-Dithyramben; Nietzsche Contra Wagner*. Berlin and Boston: Walter de Gruyter.

2016. *Nietzsche-Kommentar: Jenseits von Gut und Bse*. Berlin and Boston: Walter de Gruyter.

2019. *Nietzsche-Kommentar: Zur Genealogie der Moral*. Berlin and Boston: Walter de Gruyter.

Spencer, Herbert. 1879. *The Data of Ethics*. London and Edinburgh: Williams and Norgate.

Stern, Tom. forthcoming. 'Against Nietzsche's Theory of Affirmation'. In *Nietzsche on Morality and the Affirmation of Life*, edited by Daniel Came. Oxford: Oxford University Press.

2015. 'Against Nietzsche's "Theory" of the Drives'. *Journal of the American Philosophical Association* 1 (1): 121–40.

2016. '"Some Third Thing": Nietzsche's Words and the Principle of Charity'. *Journal of Nietzsche Studies* 47 (2): 287–302.

2017. 'Nietzsche, the Mask, and the Problem of the Actor'. In *The Philosophy of Theatre, Drama and Acting*, edited by Tom Stern, 67–87. London: Rowman and Littlefield International.

2018. 'Must We Choose between Real Nietzsche and Good Philosophy? A Streitschrift'. *Journal of Nietzsche Studies* 49 (2): 227–83.

2019a. 'History, Nature, and the "Genetic Fallacy" in *The Antichrist*'s Revaluation of Values'. In *Nietzsche and The Antichrist: Religion, Politics, and Culture in Late Modernity*, edited by Daniel W. Conway, 21–42. London: Bloomsbury.

2019b. 'Nietzsche's Ethics of Affirmation'. In *The New Cambridge Companion to Nietzsche*, edited by Tom Stern, 351–73. Cambridge: Cambridge University Press.

Sully, James. 1877. *Pessimism: A History and a Criticism*. London: Henry S. King & Co.

Volz, Pia Daniela. 1990. *Nietzsche im Labyrinth seiner Krankheit: Eine medizi-nisch-biographische Untersuchung.* Würzburg: Königshausen & Neumann.

Williams, Bernard. 2002. *Truth and Truthfulness: An Essay in Genealogy.* Princeton, NJ: Princeton University Press.

Woodward, Ashley, ed. 2011. *Interpreting Nietzsche: Reception and Influence.* London and New York: Continuum.

Acknowledgements

I presented this book at two seminars organised by Ken Gemes and Andrew Huddleston at Birkbeck College, London and at a graduate seminar at UCL. My thanks to all the participants, and to Ken and Andrew, in particular, both for organising the Birkbeck seminars and for offering detailed comments on earlier drafts. Andreas Urs Sommer shared an invaluable, unpublished draft of his commentary on *GM*. I owe a great debt of gratitude to Sebastian Gardner. I would also like to thank Ben Eggleston, Simon May, Dale Miller, Sarah Richmond and two anonymous reviewers. Finally, my thanks to Andrea Haslanger, to whom this book is dedicated.

Cambridge Elements ≡

Elements in Ethics

Ben Eggleston
University of Kansas

Ben Eggleston is a professor of philosophy at the University of Kansas. He is the editor of John Stuart Mill, *Utilitarianism: With Related Remarks from Mill's Other Writings* (Hackett, 2017) and a co-editor of *Moral Theory and Climate Change: Ethical Perspectives on a Warming Planet* (Routledge, 2020), *The Cambridge Companion to Utilitarianism* (Cambridge, 2014), and *John Stuart Mill and the Art of Life* (Oxford, 2011). He is also the author of numerous articles and book chapters on various topics in ethics.

Dale E. Miller
Old Dominion University, Virginia

Dale E. Miller is a professor of philosophy at Old Dominion University. He is the author of *John Stuart Mill: Moral, Social and Political Thought* (Polity, 2010) and a co-editor of *Moral Theory and Climate Change: Ethical Perspectives on a Warming Planet* (Routledge, 2020), *A Companion to Mill* (Blackwell, 2017), *The Cambridge Companion to Utilitarianism* (Cambridge, 2014), *John Stuart Mill and the Art of Life* (Oxford, 2011), and *Morality, Rules, and Consequences: A Critical Reader* (Edinburgh, 2000). He is also the editor-in-chief of *Utilitas*, and the author of numerous articles and book chapters on various topics in ethics broadly construed.

About the Series

This Elements series provides an extensive overview of major figures, theories, and concepts in the field of ethics. Each entry in the series acquaints students with the main aspects of its topic while articulating the author's distinctive viewpoint in a manner that will interest researchers.

Cambridge Elements ≡

Elements in Ethics

Elements in the Series

Utilitarianism
Tim Mulgan

Nietzsche's Ethics
Thomas Stern

A full series listing is available at: www.cambridge.org/EETH